D0989551

LIBRARY
OF
MOUNT SAINT MARY'S
COLLEGE
EMMITSBURG, MARYLAND

WITHDRAWN

WITHDRAWN

WHEN
THE WAR
ENDS

LIBRARY
OF
MOUNT SAINT MARYS
COLLEGE
EMMITSBURG, MARYLAND

THE TWENTIETH CENTURY FUND

TRUSTEES

A. A. BERLE, JR.

FRANCIS BIDDLE

BRUCE BLIVEN

PERCY S. BROWN

HENRY S. DENNISON

JOHN H. FAHEY

OSWALD W. KNAUTH

MORRIS E. LEEDS

ROBERT S. LYND

JAMES G. MCDONALD

WILLIAM I. MYERS

CHARLES P. TAFT

HARRISON TWEED

W. W. WAYMACK

OFFICERS

JOHN H. FAHEY, *President*

HENRY S. DENNISON, *Chairman, Executive Committee*

MORRIS E. LEEDS, *Treasurer*

EVANS CLARK, *Executive Director*

J. FREDERIC DEWHURST, *Economist*

WHEN THE WAR ENDS

DEMOCRACY UNDER PRESSURE

SPECIAL INTERESTS
VS THE PUBLIC WELFARE

Guide lines to America's future

as reported to

THE TWENTIETH CENTURY FUND

by

STUART CHASE

LIBRARY OF MOUNT SAINT MARYS COLLEGE EMMITSBURG, MARYLAND

NEW YORK

THE TWENTIETH CENTURY FUND

1945

COPYRIGHT 1945 BY THE TWENTIETH CENTURY FUND, INC.

First published January 1945
Reprinted January 1945

MANUFACTURED IN THE UNITED STATES OF AMERICA
BY E. L. HILDRETH & COMPANY, BRATTLEBORO, VERMONT

FOREWORD

Months before the United States went into the war, the Twentieth Century Fund decided to devote an increasingly large proportion of its resources to research and education on problems of postwar readjustment. As a first step, the Fund retained Stuart Chase to write a series of books to give the public his own stimulating and provocative picture of some of the questions which the United States will face "When the War Ends" (the title of the series). The entrance of the United States into the conflict has made these books even more timely. The first concern of everyone must be, of course, to win the war. But challenging objectives for the peace are dynamic aids to fighting morale. And, now that the final outcome is assured, postwar questions press insistently for answers.

The first volume of the series, *The Road We Are Traveling: 1914–1942,* was published in April 1942. In it Mr. Chase gave his colorful interpretation of the sweeping changes in our social and economic life which took place between the two world wars, and laid down a sort of base line for a preview of the future.

In the second book, *Goals for America: A Budget of Our Needs and Resources,* published in November 1942, Mr. Chase put into ringing words the needs of the American people which must be met to make a better world after the war and, using over-all figures of the goods and services these call for, he argued that we have ample man power and resources to produce them.

In *Where's the Money Coming From?*, published in November 1943, Mr. Chase carried the discussion one step further. He maintained that, not only shall we have the man power and plant to meet these postwar demands, but we shall be able to finance the full employment of our human and material resources.

But, as Mr. Chase points out in the present volume, the United States must be united in fact as well as in name if this high destiny is to be fulfilled. Treading on very specific and sensitive toes, he portrays the drift toward monopoly in business, agriculture and labor, which is preventing us from achieving the maximum volume of employment and production and he indicts the great pressure groups for threatening, even in wartime, to divide the nation by placing their own selfish economic interests above those of the public.

In the next volume, Mr. Chase will deal with questions of postwar foreign trade and investment and, in a final book, will weave the strands of the problems and solutions he has already discussed into a single pattern of challenge and hope.

This series is designed to provoke thought and to stimulate discussion. Mr. Chase has been given entire freedom of authorship and he, likewise, takes sole responsibility for all the material in this book. However, in preparing the manuscript he has had the advantage of advice and criticism from members of the Fund's staff and a number of outside consultants. But the opinions and conclusions expressed in these books are those of Mr. Chase. The Trustees and Fund staff take no position either for or against them.

In at least two closely related fields which Mr. Chase personally explores in this book — domestic monopoly and international cartels — the Fund is now conducting one of its regular major research projects. A special staff, under the joint directorship of George W. Stocking and Myron W. Watkins, is assembling the essential facts and a committee of eminent authorities will formulate a policy program on the basis of the findings.

In the field covered by Mr. Chase's *Where's the Money Coming From?* the Fund will also present the findings of professional experts: a symposium which will give the views of six leading American economists on postwar financial problems. The participants are B. M. Anderson, Professor of Economics at the University of California at Los Angeles; Howard S. Ellis, Professor of Economics at the University of California at Berkeley; Alvin H. Hansen of the Board of Governors of the Federal Reserve System; Sumner H. Slichter, Lamont University Professor at Harvard; Jacob Viner, Treasury Department adviser; John H. Williams of the Federal Reserve Bank of New York. This volume is scheduled for publication early in 1945.

The Fund hopes that all these activities will contribute to a wide public understanding both of the unequaled opportunity of the postwar period and of the difficult problems it will present. The Fund is especially indebted to Mr. Chase for his challenging contribution to this end.

EVANS CLARK, *Executive Director*
The Twentieth Century Fund

330 WEST 42D STREET
NEW YORK 18, N. Y.
DECEMBER 1944

CONTENTS

1

WILL IT BE PEACE?

The VETERANS will be coming back to Main Street to enjoy the peace. In fever-laden jungles and in the frozen north, at sea and in foxholes and in the thin high air, the men have dreamed of this return. They have dreamed of peace in prewar images, and images of fantastic Utopia. What will they find?

Main Street will not look so different to them from its prewar self, though their eyes will be sharp for changes. There is Ed's garage, and the First National Bank, and the Palace Theatre, and a fine new coat of paint on the Methodist church. Terry's meat market has gone out of business, but there is a new grocery store by the traffic light. The union hall is filled with new members and confidence; the Grange has been painted up too and seems to be coming to life. The Chamber of Commerce is staging a big drive to keep the new war plant from closing down.

The town folks will go wild when the young men come back. They will put on a parade and a carnival, and fire off the Civil War cannon in Prospect Park, the way they did in 1918. Senator Williamson will make a big speech about peace.

But will it be peace? Or will the war abroad give place to a decade of conflict at home? Will Main Street be the victim of a dangerous and bitter battle between warring pressure groups?

Will Big Business, Big Labor and Big Agriculture take up where the Germans and the Japanese left off?

Running Wild

Sometimes it almost seems so. It seemed so to Raymond Clapper just before he left on his fatal trip to the Pacific, when he wrote in his column:

> It is a sickening thing to see happening in wartime, this greedy raid all around. American men are dying all over the world, and Washington is engulfed in an obscene grab for the almighty dollar. These pressure groups are running wild. Washington is being terrorized, and every politician is fleeing for his life to fall in with the demand to break up price control.[1]

The Big Three — labor, farm, business — were the chief offenders on the price control issue. Certain labor groups were trying to crack open the Little Steel formula and thus raise wages. Farm groups were trying to kill government subsidies and thus raise food prices. Business groups were trying to kill the tax bill which was specially drawn to hold down inflation.

All this happened while the country was under fire. When victory is achieved and military patriotism is not a force — what then? That doubt was what made Raymond Clapper so bitter.

Why Nations Fall

Up to the time these words are written, in the autumn of 1944, it is significant to see which of the belligerent nations have held together under the pressures of war, and which have disintegrated. France and Italy crumbled early. Britain, Russia, Germany and Japan have taken great punishment but maintained their morale.

1. November 18, 1943.

What is the reason? Among the varying characteristics of these nations can we find a common factor of strength or weakness? It is not, I think, a question of nationality. Human beings are not so different the world around. All the men have twenty-eight chromosomes and all the women twenty-nine. The French are not less valorous than the Russians.

The ability to take it or to crack is tied up, I believe, with the way individuals feel about their country. Some folks are willing to make heavy sacrifices for their homeland, and others, just as courageous individually, are not. When the willing ones are in the majority, as in Britain or Russia, we find a nation extremely difficult to overthrow. When the willing ones are in the minority, the nation caves in.

France was cruelly split into many factions. Her government machinery was out of gear, with cabinets falling every other week. Communists, socialists, liberals, royalists, fascists, labor parties, big business, peasant blocs, rentiers, the "200 families," centrists, pro-Spanish-Loyalists, were all at each other's throats. André Mesnard writes: "Perhaps the most shocking thing brought to light by the defeat of 1940 was the bankruptcy of the elite whose task it was to unite the nation morally. When the crisis came, it was discovered that Frenchmen, in key positions, thought not as citizens of France, but as members of groups."[2]

We do not know so much about prewar opposition groups in Italy, but they are blossoming now, in many colors, in Naples and in Rome. Did Poland and Yugoslavia fail to put up much of a fight because they were torn with racial minorities?

On the Home Front

Now let us swing the pointer inward. Will the people of the

2. *The New Republic,* September 11, 1944.

United States stand firm when the test comes? The test here will spring from the aftermath of war, not from the war itself. We shall not be tried in the fires of invasion and mass bombing, but in the fires of demobilization and unemployment. We shall be tested for our ability to forge a durable peace.

We are a people with many freedoms and we glory in them. Are we so free that we lack the cement which holds a nation together in crisis? To hear us talk one would think that we could stand up to anything. The French used to talk like that too. How much of a country are we anyway? How strong is the Main Street pattern? We are going to find out before long. The furnace is being prepared and the temperature will be high. We cannot hire smart publicity men to fake our way through it. We shall have to march through it.

Taking and Giving

For three hundred years Americans have been taking from their land and natural resources without giving an equivalent back. Now almost half our arable land has been damaged or destroyed by erosion. Too many of us have thought of our country as something to be mined and exploited, not something to be loved and maintained. The people who now go to black markets with a knowing wink are carrying on the same tradition. Not only individuals but powerful groups have been operating on what might be called the Me First principle. Their eyes have not been seeing America as a whole. When they have had to choose between behaving like Americans or behaving like, say, coal miners or steel men, they have behaved like coal miners or steel men.

Time and again, the majority of Congress has lost all track of the interest of the whole community to favor the farm bloc, the Legion, the business bloc, or the labor bloc. Congressmen, pressure group leaders, administration men, the "loyal opposition," have repeatedly forsaken the clear path of what is best for the country, to follow the path of what they think is best for themselves.

For a few stirring months after Pearl Harbor we really had national unity. We buried our differences in an almost universal desire to serve the nation. Many were ready to sit up all night spotting planes, to work all day for nothing at menial jobs in hospitals, to give unlimited time as air-raid wardens and shore patrols. We were Americans all, in a dangerous world. But as the shock wore off, the unity wore off too.

By the early summer of 1943, there were days when it seemed as if the country were falling apart in a welter of strikes, crackdowns, threats, seizures, black-market operations, name-calling, bad blood, double-crossing. It was perfectly clear that those who were making the most noise were thinking about their hurt feelings, or their itch for power, or their pocketbooks, or their "competitive position."

Of course, you say; good old human nature. Then where was our human nature right after Pearl Harbor? Where do the Russians, the British, the Japanese get their devotion? Human nature is not something that goes on and off like a faucet. Again, it may be objected that pressure group politics is a good old American custom. No one can gainsay it. So was marching off to war with a squirrel rifle an old American custom. Customs change.

The Great Society

The need for developing a sense of the whole community does not arise alone from the war. We cannot operate a high-energy economy without it. As the power age advances, every man jack of us becomes more dependent on the community. Yet the community is so large that we are seldom aware of this dependence. Only when the electric power goes off in a blizzard, or the milk train breaks down, do we realize for a few minutes how the community bears us in its arms. From San Diego to Aroostook County, we are our brothers' keepers. All the Main Streets merge into one great society.

The pressure groups seem to be largely led by men who are ignorant of the fact that we are our brothers' keepers. They think such talk is Sunday School stuff. They are wrong. It is the first law of modern technology.

The self-sufficiency of the individual farmer or the small local group, which was characteristic of the handicraft age, has been sacrificed to the superior output of quantity production. Each worker, manager, establishment, now performs a single small operation in a vast national assembly line. Every citizen is dependent for his food and shelter on millions of other citizens. Nobody can go it alone any more. Your great-grandfather could get three square meals a day from his own farm, if a little salt were thrown in. Can you? Figure out where the items for a simple breakfast come from, and how many people are involved, directly and indirectly, in producing and delivering them.

The men who run pressure groups seem to assume that their crowd can go it alone. They act largely on the principle of Me First and the public be damned. If their special interest and the public interest happen to coincide, it is probable they did not plan it that way. If the public is at war, why so much the worse for the public. They talk tough and they act tough. I am not here arguing about their morals. My point is more serious. I am looking back at France in 1940, and ahead to Demobilization Day whenever it comes. I am arguing that such behavior can tear the whole economy to shreds, engulfing the tough babies with the rest of us.

Dominoes in a Row

The depression should have provided proof enough that Americans are tied together in a single organism. No group was immune as the blight spread. Even the lordly Telephone Company had to draw on its surplus account to pay dividends. Everyone went to hell in a hack — trade unionists, unorganized workers, bankers, sharecroppers, white-collar employees, architects, railroad men, teachers, writers, government employees, "widows and orphans," farmers, brokers, fishermen, artists, miners, engineers — everybody. Do you remember the empty, flyblown store windows along Main Street in 1933?

We went over like dominoes in a row without knowing what had hit us. We ought to know by this time. A high-energy society is not only inordinately productive, as Veblen used to say, it is extremely vulnerable. If the idea is every man for himself and the devil take the hindmost, the devil in no time at all works right up to the front of the line.

The pressure boys act as though they had never heard of this state of affairs. They think they can still obtain three squares a day off the old farm. They think they can kick their way through the delicate veins, nerves, tendons of an interdependent community, and get theirs. Right now they hope, most of them, if they bite hard enough in the clinches and knock over enough Congressmen, that they can claw their way up to a nice little shelf, safe from the ravages of the postwar depression.

If this spirited free-for-all actually persists after Demobilization Day, nobody will get anything, especially the rest of us. There will be no safe little shelf for anybody. With interdependence increased by $20 billion of new mass production facilities, the dominoes ought to go down even more rapidly. There will be no peace on Main Street.

It looks as if the pressure groups must either face the kind of world they are living in today, made more tenuous by the technical complexities of total war, or keep on cutting the community's life lines until somebody comes riding in on a white horse. At which point Congress becomes a memory, and pressure groups go underground for an indefinite stay. They have been underground for twenty-seven years in Russia, and for eleven years in Germany.

I am clinging to the hope that a democracy can discipline itself. Look at Britain. . . . Yes, but look at France in 1940.

2

THE WHY OF PRESSURE
GROUPS

PRESSURE GROUPS have long
been "the despair of patriots." They have been responsible for
some of the darkest days in Washington. Some of them engineered the Hawley-Smoot tariff bill, which raised so high a wall
that few imports could scale it, at a time when we were a creditor
nation. Others put over the Silver Purchase Act which made it
virtually impossible to use our great silver hoard to serve industrial wartime needs. They were responsible for the Chinese Exclusion Act. They killed bill after bill to help the consumer of
drugs and foods. They have jammed through bonus grabs, and
the totally inadequate tax bill of 1944. They continually pervert,
twist and halt the path of progress in the Republic.

Yet some sort of group representation is necessary in a democracy such as ours. Congressmen are elected on a geographical
basis. But technology has changed the meaning of geography —
and postwar airways are going to change it a lot more. Today industrial, trade, professional, wage-earning interests are often
more important than geographical. But they have no specific representation.

The pressure groups which are the despair of patriots are not a sudden calamity. They grew up with the country, like soil erosion. They are the direct result of certain economic developments and tensions.

A hundred years ago in the "atomistic society" which Adam Smith described, business units were small and fluid. I think of them as a kind of overgrown blacksmith's shop, or the village general store. My home town of Redding, Connecticut, in 1830 had seven fulling mills to bleach homespun cloth on the little streams. Today the town's one factory employs several times as many workers as all seven together.

Prices were largely determined on a free market by supply and demand. No concern was large enough to dominate the market in most things, or even influence it very much. A wide dispersal of self-sufficient family farms provided a safety net. When times were hard, a man could go back to the farm. There was always food there if one was willing to work. The age of scarcity was no Utopia, but chronic unemployment was unknown, and the ups and downs of the business cycle were not the giant roller coaster of recent years.

The first half of the 19th century was the heyday of the competitive system. Such trade monopolies as had existed earlier were broken up. The English deprived the East India Company of its monopoly in India in 1813, and in the China trade in 1833.[1] The special privileges of the old guild system were finally liquidated. Labor unions were treated as conspiracies, and ruthlessly suppressed. A few public utilities were classed as legitimate monopolies and run by the government, but private interests often operated the town water supply, the gasworks, even the roads and schools.

1. Following John Maurice Clark in his monograph on Monopoly in the *Encyclopedia of the Social Sciences,* Macmillan, edition of 1937.

Big Business

With the development of the railroads in the 1840's and '50's, a huge new industry was added to the economic system, one which was in many respects a natural monopoly. Railroads widened markets to a continental scale. Bigger markets called for bigger firms and bigger blocks of capital. The fluid atomistic society began to thicken into monopolistic lumps. The "trusts" were forming in the United States, and combinations and cartels in Europe.

The rise of technology, which had brought the locomotive, was also responsible for the large-scale refining operations which led by logical stages to the Standard Oil Company. It was responsible for other new monopolies. But sometimes trusts were deliberately formed to protect the large new capital structures against the ravages of price cutting. The U. S. Steel Corporation was organized as a kind of legal umbrella under which the companies in the combine were made reasonably immune from competitors.

Monopolistic methods were as varied as they were ingenious. By the first world war, the following could be identified:

Protective tariffs to shut out foreign competition.

The massed control of patents and secret processes.

Holding companies and mergers.

The sequestration of a limited natural resource, like copper or phosphorus rock.

The famous railroad rebate technique of Standard Oil.

The "Pittsburgh plus" formula for freight rates.

The practice of "price leadership."

Heavy advertising of brands and trade-marks, to dominate the market.

Trade associations, where little chaps could pool their strength to "stabilize" their prices.

Walton Hamilton adds more evidence:[2]

Citrus growers have turned the deliberate rotting of fruit into an established institution. The distributors of fluid milk have seized upon health regulations to throw a wall about a sheltered market. Cement dealers have fortified themselves behind a system in which a quotation to a customer runs in terms of price at a basing point, irrespective of the origin of shipment . . . and competition is powerless. . . . Oil has laid down a barrage of schemes of proration by voluntary agreement, state regulation, interstate compacts, and federal control. In paper manufacturing, the concern of the trade association is with standardizing methods in the calculation of costs; in fertilizer an open system of price filing has been used to prevent "destructive price cutting." Even the dress industry, where competition is insistent and turbulent, has attempted to subdue acquisitive zest by instigating control over design, and preventing the premature copying of cheaper dresses.

Wise old Adam Smith, even while he celebrated free competition, was aware that human nature seems to be frequently allergic to its charms. "People of the same trade," he said, "seldom meet together, even for merriment and diversion, but the conversation ends in a conspiracy against the public, and in some contrivance to raise prices." He might have been referring to the famous "Gary dinners," to be held in America a century and more later, which did so much to soften the rigors of competition in the steel business.

Industrial lobbies have been operating ever since the Republic was founded. The Constitution itself was in part a compromise among interest groups.[3] Manufacturers began pressing for tariff protection while Washington was still President. Protection and free land were the two great government handouts of the 19th

2. *Price and Price Policies,* McGraw-Hill, 1938.
3. See Charles A. Beard, *An Economic Interpretation of the Constitution of the United States,* Macmillan, 1913.

century. The hearts of Congressmen were torn with the plight of "infant industries," threatened with unfair competition from the "pauper labor" of Europe and Asia. The tariffs were granted. They were in effect subsidies which made big business bigger, and strengthened its monopolistic position. Once a tariff was granted, a lobby had to be maintained at Washington to see that it was never lowered — to say nothing of seeing what might be done about raising it higher.

A monopoly as such exerts economic pressure on the community, restricting output or holding up prices. When in addition it employs a lobby to look after its political interests, it becomes a full-fledged pressure group. In lobbying for tariffs, various monopolies often joined to form a super-group, the favorite vehicle being the National Association of Manufacturers.

Another achievement for business interests was the Supreme Court ruling that a corporation equals a man, and has all the rights and immunities of a flesh-and-blood person.

As business organizations grew after the Civil War, they gradually began to use for their support the ancient symbolism of freedom and liberty, until, in the quaint poetic fancy of our day, the United States Steel Corporation has become an individual, which must be protected at all hazards from tyranny. . . . The very Declaration of Independence is now the symbol of great business organizations, who insist that every corporation is born free and equal, and that holding companies are entitled to life, liberty and the pursuit of happiness.[4]

Big business has been pleased with this ruling. But if I am not mistaken there is trouble ahead. It is now being widely argued by the CED, Beardsley Ruml and others, that a corporation, being a legal fiction and not a person, should pay no income tax. But the

4. Thurman Arnold, *The Symbols of Government,* Yale University Press, 1935.

Supreme Court holds a corporation to be a person. The boys can hardly expect to have it both ways.

Big Labor

By the turn of the century, these large aggregations of capital had workers pretty well at their mercy. The time clock was on the wall; no longer did the master know all his men by their first names. Furthermore, it was harder to find a farm to bail into when times were hard. One-crop agriculture was undermining the self-sufficient farm. Free land in the West was about gone.

The industrial worker was on the spot. If he was not to become a helot, he had to organize a pressure group to offset the pressure of the "trusts." He did, in the person of. Samuel Gompers. The AF of L, under Gompers' dynamic direction, shed all ideological goals and concentrated on blasting out of the hands of management exclusive control of wages, hours and working conditions. The AF of L grew up with the trusts of the '90's, though several laps behind them. The railroad brotherhoods were growing too.

In due course, when their votes could really talk, labor leaders descended on the government for their own particular line of tariffs, subsidies and benefits. They wanted the legal right to organize, to picket, to strike. They wanted minimum wage laws, maximum hours, railroad retirement pensions, workmen's compensation, full crew laws, child labor restrictions, embargoes on immigrants, the exemption of unions from taxation.

Gradually the governments, state and federal, gave the unions much of what they wanted. In the Wagner Act of 1935 they got something very impressive indeed. They could now stand up and slug it out with big business. They could make even such unreconstructed antiunionists as Henry Ford and Tom Girdler bend the knee.

Observe what has happened to the atomistic society. Bargaining for wages is no longer in the hands of the free individual. It has become "collective bargaining," wherever the unions are active. The term is revealing: the free wage market has ceased to exist. Sometimes the monopolistic trend was carried a step further with the enforcement of the closed shop. So the business blocs came to represent one wing of production, the owner-managers, while the labor blocs represented another wing. The interest of all of us, as consumers, had no bloc to represent it.

Big Agriculture

The farmers were still inadequately organized when the last war came. That war boosted agricultural income, as this one is doing. Hogs, wheat and land values went over the moon. In 1920, the whole structure collapsed. In 1921, the Farm Bureau Federation organized the Farm Bloc in Congress. Thus the third major producer interest of the country became a specific pressure group.

The farmers moved on Washington, suspicious of "Wall Street" on the one hand, and "labor agitators" on the other. Beyond their own economic strength, they had two great sources of power.

In the first place, they symbolized the ancient, homely virtues — thrift, hard work, the soil, the old well sweep, the rugged independence of the great open spaces. These virtues made excellent camouflage for the hard-boiled commercial drive behind the Bloc. In the second place, the geographical election of Congressmen gave agricultural states a big mathematical advantage, especially in the Senate. Though dirt farmers accounted for perhaps a fifth of the population, they could, when organized, swing nearly half the votes in Congress.

In the 1920's, the embattled agriculturalists got a thin line of relatively cheap government credit, some assorted tariff protection, and many fine information services from the Department of Agriculture. In the 1930's, like labor, they really went to town. They got the AAA for big farmers, the FSA for little farmers, legislation for an ever-normal granary, crop insurance, farm mortgage relief, cheaper credit, the Food Stamp Plan, and many other benefits. As we shall see in Chapter 9, the Farm Bloc has engineered the major crops like cotton and corn into a position where prices are pegged and output restricted under the shelter of the federal government.

Thus large chunks of agriculture, which enjoyed — or endured, if you prefer — a maximum of free competition as late as 1932, have been hoisted clear out of the free market to become in effect state-sponsored monopolies. Historians are going to stand amazed at the rapidity of this revolutionary change in American agriculture.

Big Business, Big Labor and Big Agriculture have all organized monopolies after their fashion and left the fluid play of free competitive forces far behind them. In support of their organized economic interests, each has established powerful political lobbies to bring pressure on both federal and state governments. Political action followed economic action. The organization of labor followed the organization of business. The organization of agriculture followed both. The whole process has moved with the inevitability of a Greek drama.

The Reformers

There are no lobbies representing the whole consumer interest. The National Consumers League has been concerned chiefly with labor legislation. The Townsend Plan represents old folks, without too much regard for the rest of us. The American Legion represents veterans, with even less regard. Special groups of consumers have lobbies in Washington, some weak, some strong; but no pressure group so far as I know is looking out for all of us. Sometimes I wonder if the OPA may not prove to be the bottle from which the djinn of a real public interest group may emerge.

Beside the special interests which want something, usually with a dollar sign in front of it, for their crowd, there are the reformers. They put pressure on Congress too. Most of my readers at one time or another have been members of pressure groups out to improve the world. You may have contributed a few dollars to the Civil Liberties Union, or the Urban League, or the Planned Parenthood Association, or the League of Women Voters, or the People's Lobby. You may even have gone to Washington to join a parade, or to testify before a Congressional committee. Such lobbies have their ideological pitfalls, yet they are the hallmark of a dynamic democracy. They represent people who are not satisfied with the status quo, who want to make it a better country and are not interested in the pay-off for themselves.

The Deadly Formula

Most special interest groups have a formula which tends to freeze the economy. Not only do they want the government to interfere on their behalf, but they want a *high unit price rather than high production*. This leads straight to restriction of output, to scarcity economics, cramps and spasms.

The farm bloc fights for "parity" — the relationship of prices obtaining before the last war. The labor unions fight for high hourly rates rather than a rate of annual earnings which would keep them producing steadily throughout the year.[5] Business in-

5. The CIO is beginning to be interested in annual earnings.

terests normally have their eyes on all the traffic will bear, holding production to that level.

This is not only against the public interest, in that it keeps the national output below full employment and capacity operation, but it can be very bad business. It neglects the so-called "Ingersoll Dollar Watch formula." Ingersoll reversed the scarcity motive. He figured he could make more by selling a lot of watches at a low price, than by selling a few at a high price. Ford built up his Model T business on the same basis. It made him for a time the richest man on earth. The TVA used the formula when it set very low rates for electric power. The large volume resulting from the policy automatically decreased unit costs to the point where the low rates were profitable. As the Dollar Watch formula puts the accent always on increased production, it leads directly to high levels of employment.

Businessmen as a rule have been afraid of the high-volume–low-price idea. Perhaps it requires too much imagination. It certainly requires faith in one's product, and willingness to take a certain amount of risk. Big business would often rather play safe. Security with a regular conventional dividend is the goal. So it usually instructs its agents to campaign for relatively high prices and relatively restrained output. The whole cartel system is chained to that policy. The Ingersoll idea gets a big hand at annual banquets, but on weekdays management often takes the opposite course. So do organized labor, the farm bloc, the mining interests, and the rest.

Big Government

With the Big Three — business, labor, agriculture — all organized in an impressive way, the typical Congressman has his troubles. In a clash, whom will he support? Here is the Hon.

Clarence Cannon of Missouri, apparently requested by William Green of the AF of L to vote for the subsidy bill. Mr. Cannon searches his heart and comes up with this classic reaction: "I have always followed Mr. Green on labor bills. But this is not a labor bill. This is a farm bill. On this bill I follow the farm leaders."[6] Just when Mr. Cannon follows the welfare of the United States is not revealed.

The rise of the Big Three as outlined above warrants two conclusions. *First,* the pressure groups between them have pretty well demolished the free market as Adam Smith pictured it. *Second,* it is clear that a state dedicated to laissez faire can remain a passive umpire only so long as organizations are small. When Big Business, Big Unions and Big Farmers moved in upon the government, the community had to develop the Big State to cope with them. E. H. Carr summarizes it this way:[7]

Every modern state has intervened, first, to protect employers against trade unions, and, later, to protect the rights of the unions. If we wish to get a correct picture of the structure of the modern world, we must think not of a number of individuals . . . but of a number of large and powerful groups, sometimes competing, sometimes cooperating, in the pursuit of their group interests, and of a state constantly impelled to increase the strength and scope of its authority in order to maintain the necessary minimum of cohesion in the social fabric. . . . The issue is whether to allow social action to depend on the haphazard outcome of a struggle between interest groups or to control and coordinate the activities of these groups in the interest of the community.

This is putting the present crisis of political democracy about as flatly as it can be put. It comes down to the question of who's

6. Quoted by the *New York Herald Tribune* in an editorial, November 25, 1943.
7. *Conditions of Peace,* Macmillan, 1942.

in charge around here? If the pressure group free-for-all holds the stage, economic breakdown is not far away. If the government is in charge, there is the danger of the authoritarian state. Yet if a breakdown develops, the danger of the authoritarian state immediately reappears, and in a more extreme form.

We are not expounding theories. Even Germany was a democracy once.

3

THE PRESSURE BOYS
IN ACTION

My FRIEND Richard Neuberger, a West Coast journalist, got himself elected to the Oregon legislature a few years ago. As a new member he was fair game for lobbyists. He was waited on by a group of earnest women who wanted a law passed to restrain billboards on the highways. They were reformers interested in scenery, order and safety. The bill made sense to Mr. Neuberger and he endorsed it — just as you would, or I would. It was clearly in the public interest.

Poor innocent! The advertisers' lobby began to teach him the facts of life. Here were no fine questions of public safety and order, but a vested interest threatened with pecuniary loss. The next thing Mr. Neuberger knew, the lobby had got the Sign-painters' Union to denounce the measure and call him an "enemy of labor." This is a fearsome charge to levy against any legislator. Then came a torrent of letters from "widows and orphans" who would starve if rents from the beneficent billboard companies were cut off. Then telegrams rained in, and editorials in the papers.

The legislature ran to cover, and the bill was quashed. Mr. Neuberger believes that a large majority of the citizens of Oregon would support it, but citizens are not organized, and the lobby gets there fustest with the mostest. In the course of time the bill is certain to be passed, for it is on the trend curve; but not before a lot of beautiful country has been needlessly blighted, and a lot of cars needlessly wrecked.

Massed Battalions

Every state legislature is under similar pressure, while in Washington the heat often becomes fantastic, as Raymond Clapper sadly pointed out.

The TNEC[1] found more than four hundred lobbies in Washington — not counting the bright boy who collected $60,000 during one session of Congress by writing big executives every time a law they liked was passed, and admitting he was solely responsible.[2] We might roughly classify the four hundred into:

The Big Three — official business, labor and farm organizations, to be described in detail in later chapters.

Specialized producers, such as cattlemen, publishers, citrus growers, broadcasting stations, telephone interests.

Professional and occupational groups, such as the bankers, insurance companies, advertisers, real-estate men, exporters and importers, doctors, teachers, lawyers.

Reformers, such as the conservationists and the birth controllers.

The governments in exile, who are now protesting loudly against actual or anticipated injustices to Ruritania. Never forget that Ruritania's sons can swing a tight election in a number of Congressional districts.

1. *Economic Power and Political Pressures,* TNEC Monograph No. 26, 1941. Much of the material in this chapter came from this report.
2. Kenneth G. Crawford dug up this one in *The Pressure Boys,* Julian Messner, 1939.

What They Really Want

It is interesting to tunnel under the exalted verbiage and find the simple wants which animate some of the four hundred lobbies. For instance:

Shoe manufacturers want a higher tariff.
Farmers want parity prices.
The merchant marine wants subsidies.
So do the airlines.
The silver bloc wants 71 cents an ounce, and would take $1.00.
Teachers want federal aid.
Unions want the closed shop.
Dairymen want a prohibitive tax on oleomargarine.
Railways want to weaken the waterways and the bus lines.
Cattlemen want Argentine beef plainly labeled not fit to eat.
Insurance men do not want too much social security.
Medical men want to scuttle socialized medicine.
Coal operators want hydroelectric projects halted.
Drug men would like food and drug reformers quietly chloroformed — which would not displease the publishers either.
The aluminum interests want no nonsense at all about competitors getting hold of new government plants.

One could continue the list until it became a saga. The objective behind these wants is usually a direct subsidy for the interest itself, or a hand grenade for a competitor. Practically all the labors of the economic pressure groups revolve around these twin goals. Observe, however, that such goals are often in violent conflict as among the several groups. This is no harmony chorus.

All in the Week's Work

The TNEC describes a typical week of lobbying in the 1930's:

The American Legion pushes a war widows' pension bill through the House.

The Veterans of Foreign Wars, however, cannot get their bonus bill out of committee.

The National Federation of Federal Employees stops a pay cut in the House omnibus economy bill.

The American Automobile Association, after unheard-of efforts, fails to block a Senate increase in the automobile tax.

The petroleum lobby wangles a special tariff into the general tax bill.

The druggists' lobby — sometimes called the Pain and Beauty Boys — fights off a tax on cosmetics.

Slogans

Pressure groups make good use of slogans. The AF of L marches to legislative battle behind "The American Standard of Living." Who would be low enough to attack that? The Chamber of Commerce runs to "Free Enterprise," and the National Association of Manufacturers to "The American System." The investors' lobby works wonders with "Widows and Orphans," while the American Publishers can get away with practically anything in the name of "Free Speech and Free Press."

When a bill is to be killed, however, the accredited method is to label it "communistic," "socialistic," "fascist-inspired," "bureaucratic," "regimented," or "controlled by politicians."

All pressure groups protest that they are concerned with the "public interest." This comes as naturally to them as for a parson to declare himself against sin. They let it be known that they are making this splendid fight for the common good at great personal sacrifice to themselves. This makes it hard for the rest of us to discuss the public interest without acute nausea.

When a price-fixing job is under way, the boys call it "preventing unfair competition," or "eliminating trade abuses," or "getting rid of cutthroat competition," or "regulating chiselers." It is an awful thing to be called a chiseler. A competitive price cutter, to be sure, is the hero of Adam Smith's atomistic society. But when the Cattle Growers want to break through the OPA price ceilings in wartime, they piously advocate the "restoration of the law of supply and demand."

Strategy and Tactics

Lobbying has been going on so long that it is now almost as formal a ceremony as the tango. All the motions are known to the professional, and are endlessly repeated. Political action can take place on four fronts:[3]

First, get the "right" Congressman elected. He will vote for our bills. This means campaigning in the field.

Second, turn the heat on Congressmen already elected.

Third, influence an administrative agency to interpret bills in the "right" way. This is usually harder than influencing Congress.

Fourth, fight the constitutionality of unfavorable bills through the courts, right up to the Supreme Court. It is said that the electric power lobby used to count on an average delay of seven years after the passage of a law affecting utilities adversely, before the final decision by the Supreme Court. This gave the gentlemen quite a lot of time to turn around.

A Washington lobby normally consists of a professional agent and a staff of research workers. The agent gets up the strategy, and the research workers get up the figures. Either or both may draft the bill they want passed. Congressmen seldom prepare their own bills. The strategy is as elemental as an army's: to take more territory, and to kill off the opposition. Sometimes, as already noted, the strategy accidentally does run parallel to the pub-

3. If state governments are included, it may mean eight fronts. Also there is no limit to the backdoor pressure — persuading voters to persuade other voters to persuade politicians, and so on.

lic interest. The labor bloc lobbied for the Child Labor Amendment to the Constitution. It kept children from competing for union members' jobs, and at the same time it was a good thing for the children of the nation. The doctors have campaigned from time to time for pure food and drug legislation. The farmers have sometimes got behind conservation measures.

The agent's primary task is to build up a bloc of votes in Congress, to be backed with appeals from home at the psychological moment. This is known as "hearing from the people." The agent stands at the amplifier to megaphone the appeals. He also uses his professional abilities on the press, the columnists and the radio. His men in Congress can use their franking privilege to good advantage. A large part of the *Congressional Record* is free propaganda for pressure groups.

Congressmen are rarely influenced by debates on the floor. The best way to prove this is to take a look at them when a debate is on. Of the few who are present, those who are not reading the papers seem to be taking a nap. What really stings a Congressman into activity is (1) mail from home, (2) testimony at committee hearings, (3) high pressure from the agent.

The dangerous lobbies are not out in the open. They work in the half-light or in the dark. The techniques of entertainment, dinners, cocktail parties, subtle flattery, are often exquisite. Since the corruption law of 1911, there has not been much direct bribery. The crude buying of votes has given way to more subtle blandishments. Congressmen as well as administrative officials are shy of little black bags.

Continuity

A few lobbies operate intermittently. The Fair Trade League makes a play for fixing retail prices when in the mood. At other times it hibernates like a woodchuck. Per contra, certain manufacturers have had somebody on the job in Washington day and night for practically a hundred and fifty years. The professionals favor continuity — if for no other reason than that it stabilizes their own jobs. It gets better results than the hit-and-run method.

I once joined a pressure group to oppose the building of a reservoir in my town. The water was for Bridgeport, not for us, and there was a mean smell of a real-estate racket mixed up in the project. We were an enthusiastic crowd of amateurs, numbering such virtuosos as Franklin P. Adams, Jascha Heifetz, E. J. Steichen, the late Frank Hawks, Roger Burlingame, Louis I. Dublin, R. L. Duffus, Rollin Kirby. We worked our heads off. To hire us at space rates would have cost a million. We never got to first base. We worked only when we had the time. The water company, a private outfit, worked all the time.

A Great Big Public Uprising

When a vote is to be taken, and the moment comes to turn on the electrons, it is inspiring to watch a big lobby in operation. Constituents arrive by train, air and motor car. Sometimes they walk, or ride in buggies, or even on high-wheeled bicycles. Telegrams pour in like autumn leaves. Strong men stagger down Senate corridors under bursting sacks of mail. Editorials blossom in the local papers, duly canned for the occasion in crisp, short sentences. The wires and airwaves crackle with radio speeches and long-distance phone calls.

Young Voters' Leagues, political clubs, Independent Citizens' Committees swing into action, apparently with utter spontaneity. Movie queens, sob sisters, local celebrities get in front of flashlights. The wretched legislator is made dizzy by these activities. A big uprising, he concludes; a Great Big Public Uprising!

The agent lies low while the uprising is on. Some professionals advise getting out of Washington altogether.

A modern lobby would be unthinkable without modern technology, specifically telephone, telegraph, radio, rotogravure press and telephoto. The words often fall in the nostalgic cadences of Jeffersonian agriculture, but the technical devices which transmit these cadences are strictly up to date.

The Leader and the Led

For all this expert technical performance, it is not always clear how far the technician really represents his flock. Mr. George Gallup finds that sometimes the two are wide apart. He says:

> During recent years, polls of organized workers have, on many occasions, found them taking exactly the opposite view from the spokesmen of labor organizations. Likewise they have found farmers going contrary to the claims of their leaders, business men taking opposite views from the heads of business associations, war veterans failing to see eye to eye with American Legion officers.[4]

While labor leaders were recently fighting a bill to make unions disclose their financial condition, a poll showed 80 per cent of union members actually in favor of publicity for union accounts. Perhaps they too wanted to know where their money went.

As for mail to Congressmen, Mr. Gallup presents a striking case in connection with the Selective Service bill of 1940. As you remember, the uproar over the first draft law was prodigious. Into the offices of a group of fourteen Senators came 30,000 letters. A tabulation disclosed that 90 per cent were against the draft. Meanwhile a poll of the nation showed 68 per cent of all citizens

4. *A Guide to Public Opinion Polls,* Princeton University Press, 1944.

for the draft, 27 per cent against it, and 5 per cent with no opinion.

A skilled lobbyist has an economic interest in his job. Like the rest of us, he prefers to have it seem important. Sometimes he grows worried when the opposition weakens. He wants to give the impression of being in there swinging all the time. Thus if he is an agent for a safe-and-sane business group, he may not only welcome communist scares; he may prod the comrades a little so they will start one. If lobbies represented only the common denominator of their members, and not the personal ambitions of the lobbyist as well, they might be less of a menace.

Meanwhile, when a big campaign fills the papers and warms the airwaves, it is well to remind ourselves that a lot of the heat is synthetic.

4

PRESSURE GROUPS IN BUSINESS

The term "business" refers to so many complex activities that it must be very carefully used or it becomes meaningless. No camera could take a picture of "business."

Here we shall employ the word to mean private enterprise conducted for profit, except in farming and the professions. Although the profit is not always realized, the hope of it, or the fear of loss, usually governs the behavior of the managers who conduct the various enterprises.

Businessmen operate most of the manufacturing industries, the bulk of wholesale and retail trade, a good part of the banking, transportation, utility, construction and mining industries. Co-operatives are found in some of these activities, especially retail selling. Government is found in all of them, either as operator or regulator. But businessmen predominate.

When we generalize about "business," these are our referents. One generalization is perhaps legitimate: these organizations, so diverse in size and character, all represent a financial investment, and their managers hope to keep the investment intact and earning income over the years. Otherwise the investment is "lost," in whole or in part. Managers therefore tend to judge every political or economic change according to its probable effect in raising or lowering income. So it is quite natural for them to employ lawyers and agents and to form associations with the aim of protecting their interests and maintaining their investments.

It should also be pointed out that some of the business organizations, now to be discussed critically, contribute to the public interest by charities, scholarships, useful information services, and other collateral activities.

The National Association of Manufacturers

The heart of business pressures since the turn of the century has been the National Association of Manufacturers. So far as business-in-general has a voice, the NAM provides it. It has taken charge of matters both sacred and profane, preparing suitable ideologies, and acting with great dispatch and efficiency when a bill was to be passed or defeated.

When the TNEC published its monograph on pressure groups, the NAM included more than 3,000 corporations, employing over two million workers.[1] Through its affiliate, the National Industrial Council, which is made up of leading trade associations and local groups in the various states and cities, about two hundred and fifty in all, the NAM was said to influence 30,000 corporations, employing 5,000,000 workers. Today in 1944 there are 12,000 members, including both firms and individuals, and the National Industrial Council has 295 member associations on its list.

The NAM was organized in 1895 by a group of manufacturers in Ohio, with the special object of promoting foreign trade. By

1. TNEC Monograph No. 26, 1941.

1903 it had become a national organization and was vigorously working for the open shop. It published a pretty severe declaration of labor principles.

Its lobbying activities brought on a Congressional investigation in 1913, and the committee, somewhat awestruck, described the NAM as "an organization having purposes and aspirations along industrial, commercial, political, educative, legislative, and other lines, so vast and far reaching as to excite at once admiration and fear — admiration for the genius which conceived them, and fear for the ultimate effects which the successful accomplishment of all these ambitions might have in a government such as ours."

The investigating Congressmen were content to write a report, and the NAM proceeded on its industrial, commercial, political, educative and legislative way. In 1916 it joined with eighteen other organizations to found the National Industrial Conference Board, a highly competent research bureau which got up the figures for the business case, and still continues to do so.

From 1926 to 1933 it was not so active, but the labor legislation of the New Deal stung it into a fury of activity. By 1937, the membership had doubled over 1933. Its income in 1937 was $1,439,000, of which $793,000 was devoted to "public information." The NAM works closely with the American Bar Association, the American Newspaper Publishers Association, and with various industrial subgroups like the National Metal Trades Association.

The NAM has battled for high tariffs and for low taxes on corporations. It has fought labor unions almost from the day it was born, and "government interference" about as long. Three principles have been especially emphasized in its publicity: that taxes "hurt business"; that a protective tariff helps it; that the federal budget should be annually balanced. These are all highly respectable principles, but if the NAM were ever to retain me as consulting economist, I would undertake to prove that under certain conditions incentive taxation can be of great aid to businessmen; high protective tariffs can hurt many businesses; and that to unbalance the budget in a depression is a godsend to every business except undertakers.

The Wagner bill, setting up the NLRB in 1935, stirred the NAM to one of its finest defensive efforts. The National Industrial Council, in cooperation with the National Metal Trades Association and the American Iron and Steel Institute, manned the front-line trenches. Pamphlets, form letters, speeches, appeals for action, telegrams and long-distance telephone calls to Congressmen, were widely employed. Manufacturers were urged to go to Washington to protest in person. They were asked to install loud speakers in their plants for regular periods of propaganda each day. In spite of this determined effort, the Wagner bill was passed, and later the Supreme Court validated it.

The record of the NAM over thirty years does not show on the surface many outstanding successes, but neither does it display the more dangerous aspects of its power. The organization was pledged to keep the labor movement in its place. Never has the labor movement possessed so many members and so much power as in 1944. It was pledged to bring the virtues of the business system prominently before the public. Never did the prestige of the business system fall so low as during the depression of the 1930's.

But it would be a mistake to conclude on this account that the NAM is without influence, or weakly organized. Its organization pyramids to a tiny controlling group, which formulates policy on labor relations, business and political problems. In this group U. S. Steel, Bethlehem Steel, Standard Oil of New Jersey, and

DuPont are prominently represented.[2] The policy they dictate is relayed to member corporations, their staffs and employees; it is blown up in copious quantities of "educational" literature. The structure of the NAM is almost as autocratic in character as the average corporation itself. It lays great stress on uniformity of opinion, which of course will reflect such limitations in knowledge, tolerance and wisdom as the controlling group may have.

The Chamber of Commerce

By and large, the NAM speaks for big industry while the U. S. Chamber of Commerce speaks for the merchants along Main Street. In 1940, the U. S. Chamber represented some 1500 local Chambers, and more than 7,000 individual firm members. It has a large, dignified building right across Lafayette Square from the White House. It supports a considerable research staff, and publishes *The Nation's Business,* a vigorous weekly magazine. The 2,000 trade associations of the country tend to look to the Chamber for leadership.

It leads according to two main principles: opposition to taxes; industrial centralization controlled by businessmen themselves. The Chamber was instrumental in establishing the NRA, that early New Deal project where businessmen were to get together with their fellows in the same industry under government supervision. When for various reasons this idea turned out to be not altogether practical, its director, General Johnson, retired to write the memoirs of a very ill blue eagle. On May 27, 1935, the Supreme Court put the bird out of its misery, and the nation's most intensive experience with the cartel idea came to an end.

Next year, however, the Chamber was again advocating con-

2. Robert A. Brady, *Business as a System of Power,* Columbia University Press, 1943.

trol of industry by trade associations under government supervision. It declared that the antitrust laws should be modified to "permit agreements increasing the possibilities of keeping production related to consumption." Each industry should then be permitted to formulate and put into effect rules of "fair competition." When formulated by a clear majority of an industry, such rules "should be enforceable against all concerns in the industry."[3]

According to the TNEC, "The Chamber of Commerce approaches fiscal problems with the assumption that taxes are too high and cannot be raised further, and that therefore government expenditures must be cut if annual deficits are to be stopped." This assumption has tended to keep the Chamber in perpetual conflict with the White House and the Treasury. Government expenditures have been increasing ever since the Chamber was organized. They are estimated for the fiscal year 1944 at $98,404,000,000. Still worse, the assumption puts the Chamber in conflict with itself, for it has been an ardent supporter of government subsidies for merchant shipping and for air transport.

Assorted Industrial Lobbies

The NAM and the Chamber of Commerce are the big lobbies which speak for all business. Right behind them are a number of powerful organizations which speak for particular industries. They speak in no uncertain voice, though quite often at cross purposes.

The National Lumber Manufacturers Association has given us a frank appraisal of the function of a lobby. They believe, according to the TNEC, that geographical representation is inadequate and must give way to extra-constitutional representa-

3. TNEC Monograph No. 26, 1941.

tion through what they call the Third House of Congress. "The lobbyist of other days," says the Association, "is about extinct; the voice of the individual is little heard, and when heard has, as a rule, little influence." Government men prefer to "have the view of an industry." The individual should not bother with the personal right of petition but join a group of like-minded persons who are experts at petitioning. "An industry and its members get or do not get their dues at Washington, as they are, or are not, well represented."

The Association of Life Insurance Presidents looks out for insurance interests, and askance at social security. This insurance lobby is quiet but effective, operating mostly with state legislatures, which are even more vulnerable to pressure than Congress.

The American Iron and Steel Institute is vigorous, conservative. It is spokesman for the country's second largest industry, one which is highly organized to begin with, and which is in a key position to influence manufacturers of many products. The National Metal Trades Association, the National Coal Association, the American Petroleum Institute, the Copper Institute, are all powerful voices in Washington.

The "Lords of Creation"

The Investment Bankers Association used to be way out in front. It was established in 1912, and by 1929 had grown to a very resplendent lobby indeed. But two historical events have reduced its relative importance. The first was the Wall Street collapse, the second the abandonment of the gold standard. The Securities and Exchange Commission embodied the public reaction to the first event, tying up the practice of investment banking in a number of pretty tight knots. The second was even more serious:

America went off gold in 1933, and the last vestige of the traditional world economy vanished. Although hardly anybody discerned the deeper meaning of the event at the time, history almost at once reversed its trend. . . . Neither the League of Nations nor international *haute finance* outlasted the gold standard; with its disappearance both the organized peace interest of the League, and its chief instruments of enforcement — the Rothschilds and Morgans — vanished from politics.[4]

"Finance capital" as it was called, domiciled in Wall Street, tended to dominate industry until the collapse of the gold standard. That was the end of Wall Street's transcendent power. Governments everywhere took over the control of money and credit. Money was removed from the free market. Do you see the house of Morgan in the papers very much? Thumb back through the files before 1933 and note the enormous difference. "Generally speaking," says the TNEC, "the attitude of the Investment Bankers Association toward federal regulation of their business has been one of resignation, mingled with hope." The "Lords of Creation," as Frederick Lewis Allen used to call them, who could make or break Presidents, where are they now?

Railroads

The Association of American Railroads speaks for the railways, and normally against other forms of transportation. It is in a state of perpetual shock about government "subsidies" to bus and truck lines — specifically, letting them run free on the highways. Its protests naturally make the bus companies angry, but both may gang up on the air lines. Already the Air Transport Association is making a plea for postwar subsidies, privileges, airports and army-built transports!

4. Karl Polanyi, *The Great Transformation*, Farrar and Rinehart, 1944.

When the railroads are not fighting the bus lines, they are fighting the St. Lawrence navigation and power project, or barges on the Mississippi, or upstarts from the Far West who want what the upstarts regard as more equitable freight rates. The railroads used to fight against safety devices, but found to their surprise that safety pays in cash.

Loudly as the railroads protest subsidies to others, they have not done so badly in the subsidy line themselves. Some roads received free land — every other quarter section along their tracks in the West, to a total of 132,000,000 acres. Some received large RFC loans in the 1930's. Meanwhile, according to the tendency we described in Chapter 2, the very strength of the railroad group had stimulated the strong railroad brotherhoods, and the strong Interstate Commerce Commission. Big Business, Big Unions and Big Government are all present in this one industry.

Power

The Edison Electric Institute operates a notorious lobby. Under the style of the National Electric Light Association it had a field day during the 1920's. It set out to stop public power. "No campaign approaching it in magnitude has ever been conducted, except possibly by governments in wartime," said the Federal Trade Commission. Its advertising budget was $30 million in 1923, of which the public paid every cent through power rates. It bought up newspapers, teachers, professors, lecturers. It caused textbooks to be withdrawn, rewritten and replaced.[5] But the sad end of Middle West Utilities and Mr. Insull undermined it from one side, the TVA yardstick from another. Like the house of Morgan, the power lobby has probably seen its best days.

5. *Summary Report of the Federal Trade Commission.* Document 92, 70th Cong., 1st sess.

Ships

The merchant marine has moved from one scandal to another since the last war. It is the super-subsidy group. "No less than a dozen private fortunes have been suckled and fattened on ship subsidies," says Kenneth G. Crawford. "In the twenty years from 1917 to 1937, Congress appropriated $3,624,000,000 to build the merchant marine and pay for its upkeep."[6] In addition, $175,911,000 was paid as a bonus for carrying mail. "The subsidies which theoretically preserved the American standard of living for deck hands through the 1920's were systematically drawn off into the private accounts of the right people through complicated holding-company and service-affiliate pipe-line systems."

The industry was given, for a song, the ships built by the government in World War I. If the purchaser did not have the song he could borrow it from the Treasury at low rates of interest. He was then kept afloat by the juiciest kind of mail contracts. In 1936, the whole odoriferous mess was aired, and the American Merchant Marine Institute replaced the salty and tarred American Steamship Owners Association. But pressure groups do not always sprout wings when they are called "institutes." From now on the movements of this particular Institute will be worth watching. We are coming out of this war with the United States government owning perhaps two thirds of the merchant tonnage of the world, according to Admiral Emory S. Land. That is enough to make any Institute's mouth water.

Possibly even this tonnage will not satisfy the merchant mariners. Already they are looking aloft to the air lines. "The steamship industry maintains," writes the Institute's president, in a de luxe 278-page issue of the *Marine News,* "that it is better fit to operate those services than companies which engage solely in the

6. *The Pressure Boys,* Julian Messner, 1939.

business of air transportation." The Air Transport Association may be expected to disagree violently.

Tin and Silver

Tin was a critical war material. The Japanese cut off the main supply in Malaya, and we had no refinery capacity in this country. Tin from Bolivia had to be shipped to Britain to be refined, then back to the States for plating, twice crossing the path of the U-boats. Sometimes it crossed a third time, when it was lend-leased abroad. But we had plenty of silver. Silver could take the place of tin in the manufacture of parts for ships, tanks, trucks, guns, shells, bombs and torpedoes. The production men were begging for it. There were 1,361,000,000 ounces of silver bars in the vaults of the Treasury, invaluable for the war effort. The world market price was about 35 cents an ounce, which would have met the situation nicely. But the Silver Bloc in Congress had fixed it so that the Treasury must pay 71 cents an ounce for all silver mined in the country, and could not sell its bars for less than $1.29 an ounce.[7] Wars may come and go, but the Silver Senators never lay down their muskets.

Houses

It is almost universally agreed that housing can be the largest single outlet for employment after the war. It was one of the greatest after the last war. But it will be a pretty slim channel if the building lobby has its way. Its formula is for the government to assume all the risks, while private builders get all the profits. Through FHA and HOLC, the federal government now owns one out of every six mortgages. "This is a new socialization of land. In the planning for rebuilding blighted areas a strange

7. Editorial in *The New York Times,* September 27, 1942.

type of nationalization is advocated, in which the real estate is controlled by private groups, but the government puts up all the money. The stakes are very big."[8] This sounds like the beginning of another super-subsidy program.

There is a good chance that the postwar housing program, with its millions of jobs, can be deadlocked. The probability that the real-estate men will lose out, too, is small solace against the loss of employment for the rest of us. A few of them are pleading for a more enlightened approach, in which government and industry work out the housing program together. But so far they are in the minority.

Drugs and Cosmetics

In 1937, more than seventy people were killed by a proprietary remedy, marketed by one of the patent medicine fraternity with less than their usual care.[9] The Pain and Beauty Boys do not want to kill people, but they are normally in a hurry. In 1934, when the Copeland bill for pure food and drugs was introduced to slow them down a little, an impressive lobby was summoned against it. The leader was the Drug Institute, founded by the Walgreen interests. Under its banner marched the National Drug Trade Conference, the National Association of Retail Druggists, the National Wholesale Druggists Association, the Institute of Medicine Manufacturers, the Allied Manufacturers of the Beauty and Barber Industry, Inc., to say nothing of several leading law firms.

The National Publishers Association, which represents the "slicks," the National Editorial Association, which represents the weeklies, and the American Newspaper Publishers Association

8. Charles Abrams, Speech before the League for Industrial Democracy, May 8, 1943.
9. Helen Woodward, *It's an Art,* Harcourt, Brace, 1938, p. 189. See also Crawford's reference in *The Pressure Boys.*

made the welkin ring with alarm and grief that such things as the Copeland bill could be. "Generally speaking, the drug crowd took care of the newspapers, and the canners delivered the women's magazines." E. L. Bernays, working for the lobby, produced a "Joint Committee for Sound and Democratic Consumer Legislation," and to make assurance doubly sure, a "National Advisory Council of Consumers and Producers."[10] The bill was eventually passed on the momentum of the New Deal, but you would hardly have recognized it as finally watered down.

This is the baldest illustration of the Me First principle I know of. The public interest is plain enough for an intelligent dog to see. Not only pill manufacturers and depilatory makers attack this interest, but the massed power of the press as well — dailies, weeklies, monthlies, every medium which carries patent medicine and cosmetic advertising. They attack of course in the name of freedom and liberty. They attack a proposal which would make it illegal to poison people, or to delude them into buying a cure which cannot cure them.

Five Conclusions

One could go on citing evidence collected from literally thousands of pages of Congressional hearings. The Federal Trade Commission's investigation of the power lobby fills many volumes. I can give here only the briefest indication of the documented material available.[11] But perhaps we can summarize the major conclusions from the evidence as follows:

1. The business pressure groups, in most cases, have been oblivious to the public interest.

10. Kenneth G. Crawford, *The Pressure Boys,* Julian Messner, 1939.
11. In *Your Money's Worth,* Macmillan, 1927, F. J. Schlink and I presented some substantial evidence.

2. They have been pretty well devoid of responsibility, not only to the public but to their own consumers and their own workers. Their corporate financial interest has been the major objective.

3. Many business lobbies are pressing for monopolistic advantages, or a subsidy, or both. In such cases pretty speeches by their pressmen about "free enterprise" become a complete contradiction.

4. Except on a high ideological level, there is none too much unity among the business groups. They are constantly in each other's hair in the practical matter of the division of the national income.

5. If the little independent businessman is going to survive, it looks as if he had better climb aboard a powerful trade association. Everybody else has a grateful tear for him, but nobody is going to do much of anything for him.[12] Big business is coming out of the war bigger than ever.

To the economic rather than the political activities of big business we will now address ourselves.

12. With the possible exception of Maury Maverick.

5

BIG BUSINESS

W E HAVE SEEN some of the organizations through which business establishments can exercise political power. But to exercise economic power many a large business needs no lobby at Washington. Its sheer weight creates economic pressure, especially if it happens to be the giant in its field.

Instead of indulging in easy generalizations about Big Business we should remind ourselves that the term is relative and the scale a gradual one. Suppose the Internal Revenue Bureau showed you a great table, listing the taxable income of all the business enterprises in the nation, from the largest to the smallest. You look down the thousands of figures, each deviating only slightly from the next. Where would you draw a line and say: Here "big business" ends and "little business" begins? Wherever you put your line, it is safe to say that big business would be divided from little business by something in the nature of eighty-nine cents.

The Department of Commerce utters a short prayer and brings down the pointer at net sales of $199,999.99 or less for small business in wholesaling, net sales of $49,999.99 or less in retailing, a pay roll of 100 employees or less in manufacturing. On this basis, there are 2,800,000 little businesses in the country.

Another indication of bigness and power is "the frequency of 'plural units' — combinations in which more than one industrial establishment is operated by a single central office. In 1929 . . . only about one eighth of the manufacturing enterprises were of the plural unit type, but this small fraction accounted for about 48 per cent of the wage earners, 54 per cent of the value of the products and 50 per cent of the value added by manufacture of all manufacturing enterprises."[1]

"Monopolistic Competition"

"Monopoly" is synonymous with big business in many people's minds, and "free competition" with little business. Here again there is no clean-cut line where monopoly ends and competition begins. In recent years a considerable literature has grown up about a state of affairs called "monopolistic competition."[2] Under this theory, most production is carried on in an area between the two poles of perfect competition and perfect monopoly. In perfect competition three conditions must be met: (1) a large number of small sellers, (2) who sell a homogeneous product, in (3) a market where newcomers have free entry. Monopolistic competition exists where one or two of these conditions are absent. Free competition establishes an equilibrium at maximum output, but monopolistic competition, according to the theory, leads to a balance at lower levels, say at 80 per cent of capacity, or 60 per cent.

Certainly at one end of the scale, great enterprises like the Aluminum Company, or the U. S. Post Office, can be called monopolies without much qualification, while at the other end, cleaning and dyeing shops along Main Street, engaging in sanguinary price

1. Alfred Bernheim and others, *Big Business: Its Growth and Its Place,* The Twentieth Century Fund, 1937.
2. For instance: E. H. Chamberlin, *The Theory of Monopolistic Competition,* Harvard Economic Studies No. 38, 1933.

wars, can be called truly competitive. In between are all manner of quasi-monopolies, and more or less tainted competitive markets.

Practically all big businesses have monopolistic elements, if for no other reason than the large amount of capital a competitor would need to crash into them. But a number of little businesses in a given field may combine in a trade association, which can give them a very pretty monopoly. The control goes to the leader of the association, who may be the largest producer, as in the classic case of the Newsprint Manufacturers Association;[3] or even to an outside organizer — say a firm of efficiency engineers, as in the case of paper-box manufacturers cited by Thurman Arnold.[4] The trade association uses its power almost always to fix prices, sometimes through collusive bidding, as practiced by dealers in building supplies.

What is a monopoly? Let us define it as a situation where competition in that industry need not be greatly feared. Competition is always to be feared from another industry, or from a new invention. Thus the steel industry fears the new light metals, and the automobile industry fears a cheap, foolproof airplane. Retailers of various kinds fear the versatile druggist, who competes with everyone, from grocer to bookseller.

"Cartel" has two meanings: as a synonym for monopoly, and, more usually, as a monopoly which has become international.

The Match Business

As industries go, the manufacture of matches is not very great, but it presents a tidy picture of a situation where competition need

3. Harry Laidler, *Concentration of Control in American Industry*, Crowell, 1931.
4. *The Bottlenecks of Business*, Reynal and Hitchcock, 1940.

not be much feared. The Department of Justice has recently spread upon the record the following facts:[5]

The Diamond Match Company controls the five largest match manufacturers in the United States. These five companies control 83 per cent of U. S. production. Eleven companies, including the American five, with two British, one Canadian, and three Swedish (shades of Ivar Kreuger), control 75 per cent of the match business of the planet. The U. S. monopoly thus belongs to an international cartel.

As a cartel, the eleven companies have divided up the world market, carefully keeping out of one another's domain. Diamond refused to sell Latin America, it is alleged, either matches or match-making machinery — of which Diamond also has an American monopoly. This was in deference to the Swedish companies, whose backyard Latin America was, according to agreement.

A European inventor devised a "repeating" match which could be scratched, blown out, and scratched again, 140 times in a row. This dream match would be to smokers what the technocrats' everlasting razor blade would be to shavers. The cartel bought the invention and gave Diamond the American rights. Diamond promptly suppressed it. According to the files of the company, the invention was "a distinct danger to the American match industry, and would be a fertile field for the rottenest kind of competition."

Remember that phrase — "the rottenest kind of competition." We shall return to it shortly. It symbolizes a far-reaching and dramatic conclusion about the modern economy. Meanwhile Diamond Match is no better and no worse than most other big companies which dominate their industries.

5. *Time*, May 8, 1944. The facts are of course disputed by the defendant.

Classes of Monopolies

Thurman Arnold, who has probably tangled with more monopolies than any other man alive, divides them into four major classes.[6]

1. The control by a single company of the entire output, except as it allows a few small fry to operate on good behavior. He cites as examples the United Shoe Machinery Corporation and the Aluminum Company of America. These are old-fashioned, aged-in-the-wood "trusts," the kind that agitated Theodore Roosevelt.

2. The control of an industry by a few large companies under an arrangement where competition keeps nobody awake nights. They decline to compete in price, but wage furious battles in five colors in *The Saturday Evening Post,* and have a good deal to say at $5,000 a page about their superior services to the consumer. The oil industry and the automobile industry are examples. Executives of such companies look hurt if anyone calls them monopolists, so someone has coined the word "oligopoly" to make them feel better. This would also be a case of "monopolistic competition" under the definition cited earlier.

3. The control of a distribution line in which every newcomer is forced to pay tribute to the system. Plumbing fixtures are an example. "This system requires an elaborate organization of manufacturers, jobbers, master plumbers, journeymen plumbers, with a labor union as its front line of defense." The idea is to prevent those with better fixtures from ever getting anywhere near a house. This is why there has been little improvement in the mechanism of flush toilets for fifty years. Note that this monopoly consists of "big business," plus "little business," plus labor unions. The type is common throughout the building trades.

6. *The Bottlenecks of Business,* Reynal and Hitchcock, 1940.

4. The "Chinese bandit system" of restraint of trade in unorganized industry, found notoriously in food and fuel distribution. The small operator pays for "protection." The toll of such rackets in New York or Chicago alone has been enormous.

The techniques for seizing and maintaining monopolistic advantage are legion. Outstanding methods today are control of patents and patent pools, protective tariffs, ownership of a limited natural resource, holding-company devices, and sheer size. Let us follow Walton Hamilton in his inspection of a patent monopoly.[7]

Patent Pools

The Hartford-Empire makes nothing at all. It is a company composed of filing cases and abstruse legal concepts. It has got hold of most of the patents on the making of glass bottles, containers and bottle-making machinery. When the patents expire it knows how to prolong protection. If the article is air with some glass around it, that is Hartford's dish. To get into the bottle business is tougher than getting into Skull and Bones. You have to be tapped. When admitted, you must obey all the club rules. You are told what kind of bottles you can make, where, when, and for how long. You are told in what territory you can sell them. Your capacity, your rate of output, the price you shall charge, are all engrossed on the bond.

One little slip, my boy, and Hartford will yank you into court for infringement of patent. Do not imagine they will fail to notice it. "In respect to law enforcement, no sovereign state in the union can compare with Hartford-Empire in the matter of police. It is not a state-within-a-state, it is a little too late to say that. It is a state-elect. . . ." Whatever it is, it is a honey.

7. Address to People's Lobby Conference, Washington, February 12, 1944. See also Thurman Arnold, *op. cit.,* on Hartford-Empire.

When the old mammy songs about free enterprise come over the airwaves, I shut my eyes and think of all the bottles in all the milk wagons of the Republic, and all the canning jars in all the kitchen cupboards, every last one of them compounded of silica, potash and a permit from Hartford-Empire.

The patent law had the estimable purpose of protecting the inventor, and encouraging technology. Now big business concerns seem to have annexed the law and run it as a profitable subsidiary. Their engineers get up minor improvements and their lawyers patent them, until a given manufacturing process is surrounded with legal barbed wire. Nobody can get into it, any more than the Germans could get into Moscow. Said the president of a large titanium company: "The whole purpose of the cartel is to obtain a monopoly of patents so that no one can manufacture titanium except the members of the cartel, and so can raise prices by reason of such monopoly to a point that would give us much more profit on our present tonnage."[8] A good, forthright statement.

Wendell Berge of the Antitrust Division reports in *The New York Times:*[9] "There is no opportunity for a new company no matter how great its resources to manufacture: An electric lamp, a glass bottle, an aluminum pot, a pair of spectacles, any vitamin product, a radio set, or numerous other things which form a part of our daily lives."

Controlled Markets

Skipping to another quarter of the industrial front, we come upon a great drum of American cheese. Cheese is produced by

8. Reported by Robert Reuben in *The New Republic,* February 14, 1944.
9. September 26, 1943. There is some evidence that the vitamin monopoly has since been dented, if not broken.

hundreds of small fry, including many farmers' cooperative associations. These sell to middlemen, who warehouse the cheese and sometimes process it. Six companies do 82 per cent of the warehousing. The price is based on certain rites performed weekly at Plymouth, Wisconsin. Remove your hats, for we are standing in the presence of the Market. Let Mr. Arnold draw aside the curtain.[10]

Borden bids 15 cents for Swift's lot; Swift bids 15 cents for Kraft's offering; Kraft bids 15 cents for Armour's offering, and so on for a few thousand pounds of cheese. Word then goes out on the wires to all parts of the United States that the price of cheese on the Plymouth Exchange is 15 cents a pound. Now comes a significant part of the whole transaction. This price, determined in such a gentlemanly manner at Plymouth, becomes the basic settlement price for millions upon millions of pounds of cheese bought and sold throughout the U. S. If this hocus-pocus was limited to cheese, the farmers and the consumer might survive. As a matter of fact, the same situation applies in a greater or lesser degree to a multitude of farm products.

The four leading companies in the following industries control:[11]

> 97 per cent of the national production of asbestos shingles
> 92 per cent of tractors
> 90 per cent of automobiles
> 89 per cent of cultivators
> 85 per cent of window glass
> 83 per cent of rubber overshoes
> 80 per cent of dry batteries
> 79 per cent of harvesting combines
> 79 per cent of kerosene stoves
> 77 per cent of refrigerators

10. *The Bottlenecks of Business.* Mr. Arnold does not imply, of course, that all markets are rigged like cheese.
11. *Competition and Monopoly in American Industry,* TNEC Monograph No. 21, 1940.

When depression hits a relatively free market, prices fall head-long, but production may be maintained in an attempt to get as much gross income as possible. When it hits a monopolized or controlled market, the opposite happens: production is deliberately cut way back, employees are fired, and prices are maintained. Observe this principle at work in the first years of the depression:

Changes from 1929 to 1932 in the free markets

Corn	the price fell 67%;	production increased 15%
Cotton	" " " 66%;	" decreased 12%
Cottonseed oil	" " " 60%;	" increased 5%
Oats	" " " 57%;	" " 11%
Tobacco	" " " 57%;	" " 5%
Wheat	" " " 59%;	" decreased 8%

In the monopolized markets for the same period

Aluminum . . .	the price fell 4%;	production decreased 41%
Automobiles . .	" " " 11%;	" " 76%
Sulphur	" " " 0%;	" " 62%
Cultivators . . .	" " " 3%;	" " 90%
Iron ore	" " rose 1%;	" " 93%
Plate glass . . .	" " fell 5%;	" " 65%
Steel rails	" " " 1%;	" " 85%

The Brimstone Game

Professor R. H. Montgomery, who gives us these figures,[12] has this to say about the sulphur monopoly:

In competitive industry, prices usually stay within hailing distance of production costs. . . . There is no better evidence of monopoly than a continuous and long-maintained level of prices well above production costs. In the brimstone game there is no apparent affinity between the two! For more than thirty years sulphur prices have been about three times production costs. For two periods of more than a

12. In his book, *The Brimstone Game; Monopoly in Action*, Vanguard, 1940.

decade each, prices have been held absolutely rigid at $18 per ton, while the best estimates of costs varied from $3.48 to $6.79 per ton.

In the early 1930's a Norwegian company developed a process for extracting pure sulphur from pyrites. Pyrites are found all over the map. Here was a serious challenge to the cartel! "For a quarter century one, two or, at most, three American companies had held an effective, stable, and quite profitable world monopoly." The cartel moved in on the Norsemen like Hitler's legions crossing the Skagerrak. When the shooting was over, the Norsemen were nailed down to do business only in the Baltic, the cartel had the patents for the Western Hemisphere, and the price of sulphur continued serenely at $18 per ton.

Locking Up Invention

Fortune gives us a list of recent new developments suddenly stopped in their tracks:[13]

An asbestos-concrete steel-lined pipe for oil pipe lines. (It needs only 15 per cent as much steel as the usual type.) Stalled by the opposition of the seamless-tube industry.

Aluminum from common clay. Research projects vetoed by ALCOA men on government committees. The Bureau of Mines' project was also blocked.

The development of equipment to aid quick-freezing stations for frozen food. Opposed and killed by the canners, the container manufacturers, and the big food processors.

A flour milling process that produces white flour plus vitamins, without rancidity. Savage opposition from big millers, committed to the enriched bread program, locked it up.

There are many more cases like this, says *Fortune*. We might call them refinements in the art of industrial strangulation.

13. "The Bottleneck in Ideas," May 1943.

Extent of Monopoly

Berle and Means estimated in 1930 that two hundred non-financial corporations controlled half the industrial wealth of the United States.[14] This would indicate that they had a commanding voice in determining the quantities and prices of half the goods we buy. A recent estimate shows one hundred nonfinancial corporations receiving 70 per cent of war contracts — some of which they subsequently sublet.

These great companies are not all monopolies, but with such heft they can hardly avoid dominating their respective industries. The worthy young enterpriser, starting like an Alger boy from one suspender, has quite a task before him in accumulating the $20 million, or the $100 million, or whatever the necessary kitty is, to break into such a business.

The war has not only increased the size of individual corporations,[15] but in some cases has integrated a whole industry as a co-operative unit. Thus the automobile industry has pooled all tools and machines, with free transfer from plant to plant. Contract information and technical information are similarly pooled throughout the industry. Production problems and "know-how" are discussed in joint meetings. The industry's brilliant success in war production is largely due, in my opinion, to these practices combined with guaranteed government orders, rather than to the beauties of free enterprise.

Integration has also taken place in other industries. It will doubtless continue in some form after the war. The implications for monopoly control are staggering.

14. *The Modern Corporation and Private Property*, Macmillan, 1933.
15. C. F. Hughes in *The New York Times*, August 6, 1944, cites the metalworking industries. "Plants employing 2500 workers or more in 1939 produced approximately 22 per cent of the nation's shipments; in 1943 they ran well over 55 per cent."

Little Business

Meanwhile little business shrinks relatively as big business grows. The looming problems of reconversion are having a particularly bad effect on small businesses. They have had little chance to accumulate reserves to carry them over the transition period. Their equity in new war plants is narrower than that of big business, and their ratio of working capital to total liabilities is less. They are beginning to see the end of their 20 per cent annual depreciation allowances, and operators of small business fear that the allowances will expire just when contract cancellations hit them.

As I write, a tug of war is developing in the WPB as to the order in which companies reconvert to peace, and the proportion of business they acquire. The big boys want the ratio frozen on the 1940 basis; each company to resume its prewar quota. This would shut out new companies altogether — such as Kaiser's steelworks on the Coast. Another group is said to favor admitting new companies if they are competent to turn out the goods. Watch this fight. *It will probably determine the fate of little business in this country for the next generation.* If the prewar quotas are frozen and enforced, "Free enterprise" can probably be laid away in lavender, along with "Fifty-four forty or fight," "Free silver," and other historical slogans.

Tono Bungay

The impact of monopoly on society has rarely been better illustrated than in H. G. Wells' *Tono Bungay*, which, like a good cartoon, drives home a complicated point with an economy of means. The hero has just listened to his uncle, who keeps a small chemist's shop, develop a scheme for monopolizing quinine and making a million:

The idea of cornering a drug struck upon my mind then as a sort of irresponsible monkey trick that no one would be permitted to do in reality. . . . I thought it was part of my uncle's way of talking. But I've learned differently since. The whole trend of modern money-making is to foresee something that will presently be needed and put it out of reach, and then haggle yourself wealthy. Of course the naïve intelligence of a boy does not grasp the subtler developments of human inadequacy. He begins life with a disposition to believe in the wisdom of grown-up people; he does not realise how casual has been the development of law and custom. He thinks that somewhere there is a power as irresistible as a head master's to check mischievous and foolish enterprises. I will confess that when my uncle talked of cornering quinine, I had a clear impression that anyone who contrived to do that would pretty certainly go to jail. Now I know that anyone who could really bring it off would be much more likely to go to the House of Lords!

Mr. Wells wrote his famous novel in 1909, but in 1940 the quinine cartel was in a position to do just what our hero's uncle was dreaming of. The result, though more impersonal, was no less evil than Mr. Wells imagined.

The evil is not so much the money such a concern makes as its total lack of responsibility to the society which grants it a charter, enforces its contracts, and protects its property. Restriction of output is the one thing a dynamic society cannot long tolerate.

6

ARE MONOPOLIES
INEVITABLE?

Nobody has ever estimated, or can estimate, the percentage of the total economic activity of the nation which has been lifted out of the free market. We know that the percentage had been growing steadily up to the war. We have seen how the war has increased the share of the big chaps against the little chaps — which furnishes a strong presumption of growing monopoly.

We know that free competition has been declining in many parts of the world even more rapidly than in America. Throughout the vast domain of Russia it has altogether gone, except for some "socialist competition" between the state trusts. Throughout much of Europe free competition has been practically obliterated by the Nazis, while the returning governments-in-exile seem to be pledged to planned economies.

No other countries have antitrust laws such as our Sherman and Clayton Acts. Many foreign governments not only encourage international cartels, but participate in them. Powerful cartels are now said to be hibernating in Switzerland, getting ready for action the instant the war ends.[1]

1. W. V. Archawski, "Switzerland, Foster Mother of Cartels," *Harper's Magazine,* September 1943.

This state of affairs is not only extraordinary in the light of the current crusade for "free enterprise" in America, it is even more extraordinary in the light it throws on human beings and their institutions. Many of us seem to take to monopoly like a sailor to beer. Many of us, like the officers of the Diamond Match Company, look on competitors as a danger to our business, and denounce the repeating match, or whatever the new process is, as providing the "rottenest kind of competition."

Assuming it to be technically legal, without secret rebates and the like, when is competition "sound" and when is it "rotten"? Is there anything in the philosophy of laissez faire to allow for such a distinction? There is not. The distinction occurs first in the mind and then in the behavior of most businessmen. We are getting down to bedrock here. Is there something in human nature, or in the structure of human society, which makes monopolies under certain circumstances inevitable? The whole postwar world is waiting for an answer to that question. The future of business enterprise is tied up with it.

Legal Monopolies

To clear the ground, the question has already been answered in the affirmative so far as legal monopolies are concerned. Certain industries have been declared monopolies, affected with a public interest, and are operated or regulated by the state. For instance, government runs the post office and regulates the telephone company. You would go crazy with half a dozen competing telephone companies running a line into your house. The cost per call meanwhile would be many times what it is under monopoly conditions. Water, gas, street railways, electric power, radio airwaves are legal as well as technological monopolies.

Only a fanatic like Herbert Spencer or Isabel Paterson would atomize these technological unities. Their prices are often fixed — as the Interstate Commerce Commission fixes railroad rates; their new investments are controlled, their conditions of service specified. Thus a considerable and growing section in the economy is already posted "Monopoly — Keep Out. This Means You." This section has been taken off the free market by the march of technology and by common consent, and handed over to the community to be controlled in the interest of all the people.

The Tendency of Enterprisers

But how about matches, cheese, automobiles, tractors, milk bottles, plumbing fixtures, as we looked at them in the last chapter? In America, such goods are supposed to be sold in the free market. The cheese business goes through all the motions of a free market. Why have these industries and many others ceased to be genuinely competitive? Why is there a constant, cumulative drive to take them out of the free market?[2]

Beardsley Ruml used to teach psychology before he became a merchant prince. He says in his excellent little book, *Government, Business and Values:*

> The tendency of enterprisers is constantly to create situations tending toward exclusiveness or monopoly, either as buyer or seller; whereas collectively . . . as applied to all others except themselves, the benefits of competition are clearly recognized.

Barbara Wootton, a shrewd and irreverent critic, observes that it does not take profound insight to discern the advantages of monopoly.[3] Since a monopolist is always in a more advantageous position than a competitor among competitors, it follows that

---

2. It is true that a reverse drive is also at work, where monopolies are broken into and dissolved by strong competitors, but it is the weaker of the two.
3. *Lament for Economics,* Allen and Unwin, 1938.

there is considerable *instability* about the state of competition, and an inherent tendency for competitive markets to become monopolized. If a businessman is intelligent enough to grasp the logical beauties of free competition, he is intelligent enough to grasp the superior advantages of monopoly. "Experience has shown," says Miss Wootton, "how persistent is the threat of monopoly to competition, and how difficult it is to keep alive a competitive regime by any kind of artificial respiration."

The literature of "monopolistic competition," to which we referred in the preceding chapter, is an attempt to explain this apparent contradiction. Even Adam Smith himself, practically at the cradle of laissez faire, noted sadly how businessmen could not sit down to a friendly round of drinks without hatching conspiracies in restraint of trade.

When I was a practicing accountant, I observed that my clients were often moving in the direction of controlling the market. I was a kind of midwife at the birth of several partial monopolies and mergers; at least I prepared the consolidated balance sheets.

Is the Antitrust Division of the Department of Justice an exhibit in artificial respiration? How much free competition can be re-established by government strong-arm methods? Thurman Arnold, threatening prosecution under the Sherman Act, used to get the monopolistic gentlemen to sign consent decrees, by which they promised to be less monopolistic. But among their friends they called this procedure "governmental blackmail."

Professor J. M. Clark believes that it would require a larger amount of "government interference" to enforce free competition than any other course we might follow. He sees no chance of a real return to laissez faire.[4] Professor T. O. Yntema doubts if we can have a massive world-trend toward planned economy and

4. *Journal of Political Economy*, December 1941.

a successful domestic drive for free competition, at one and the same time.[4] "Eventually," he says, "the anti-monopoly campaign is likely to recede in importance, because it is less deeply rooted in our social and political structure. . . ."

Paradox

This is all very perplexing, for the small competitive businessman, full of initiative and self-reliance, is very deeply rooted as a symbol of the American system. True, it becomes increasingly difficult to find such men in the flesh, but even as their numbers shrink, the aura about the symbol grows. They have been called the "yeast of the economy." The current celebration of free enterprise is directed toward the sturdy competitor as the savior of society. Yet while we celebrate, the big boys grow bigger on war orders and the government reaches out further.

To suppose that competition and monopoly are natural opposites is absurd, says C. E. Ayres.[5] It is the ambition of every competitive businessman to put his rivals out of business and absorb their trade. Ten days' apprenticeship in a competitive enterprise, he says, should convince any inquiring student of the true nature of competition.

The NRA, most of us agree, was a very wicked piece of legislation. It sought to make American industry a series of cartels under government supervision. It left no place for the venture capital man at all. We thanked God when the Supreme Court declared the law unconstitutional; but was it, or was it not, closer to the trend curve of the real, wicked, workaday world than the current ideological crusade?

It is, I repeat, a strange paradox, this proliferation of monopoly

5. *The Theory of Economic Progress*, University of North Carolina Press, 1944.

in the teeth of what all the good books, the good professors, the good corporation presidents, and the good Congressmen have been saying for a century and more. It is like the war against sin. The preachers thunder every Sunday, but the congregation loses so much ground during the other six days that the preachers never can catch up.

In our perplexity let us turn to the economic historian Karl Polanyi. He has a theory which tries to explain the enigma. After a superbly documented analysis, he concludes that the formation of monopolies was due not so much to human waywardness as to a revolt of society against the stony rigors of the automatic market. Let us briefly examine his thesis, for it may help us in trying to find an answer to the paradox.[6]

The Great Transformation

Polanyi describes how the market economy started with bright Utopian promises, and how by subordinating everything to a maximum output of goods, its leaders hoped to solve mankind's economic problems. He traces the steady deterioration of that ideal until the final collapse of the world free market in the early 1930's, and the adoption of managed economies by every state on earth.

Why did such a logical conception come to such a sad end? Polanyi is the first, as far as I am concerned, ever to answer this question satisfactorily. *The chief trouble with the Market, he says, was not that it exploited people — which of course it did from time to time — but that it dissolved society.* It broke up the family and made people spiritually homeless. It wrenched them out of their farms, their crafts, their ancient ties, and herded them, rootless, into the dark, Satanic mills. It offered a mechanical in-

6. *The Great Transformation*, Farrar and Rinehart, 1944.

stitution depending on money prices to supersede the organic human institutions which mankind had always known. For thousands of years, markets had been dependent on society, defined in this sense. Men came first and money second. The 19th century reversed the process, and the resulting tensions finally exploded in the disorders, wars, revolutions of our time. The more one thinks over this hypothesis, the more impressive it becomes.

The era of mercantilism, which preceded the Market, was one of expanding trade routes, but they were controlled by the state, often elaborately controlled. At the time of the industrial revolution, the middle classes revolted against these controls. Their revolt was so determined that it swung the pendulum all the way over to the ideal of no control at all. Instead of a series of little regulated markets set against the background of organic society, there was to be one big Market, self-regulating and automatic, to which all social behavior should be subservient.

Everything a Commodity

In order to have a truly self-regulating and flexible system, Polanyi points out, everything must obviously be included, because everything must be treated as a commodity with a price. Otherwise the mechanism will not work automatically. Labor must become a commodity; so must land; so must money. As a result, industrial workers, with nothing but the Market to depend upon, were stripped of human dignity, to be disposed of like so much pig iron. Their less negotiable qualities tended to disappear. Similarly the buying and selling of natural resources, removed from the ancient protection of society, amounted to summoning the demons of flood, fire, erosion, dust storm, stream pollution.

Money was made a commodity by tying it to gold. Gold was

bought and sold like anything else, at so much an ounce. Its behavior was naturally uncertain, with alternate gluts and shortages. This caused recurring shocks to the money supply, and threatened the stability of industry. Businessmen, according to Polanyi, were the first victims of the money-commodity theory. "The Market required that the individual respect economic law even if it happened to destroy him."

Society versus the Market

Almost immediately society moved to protect itself against this logical Moloch. The first reaction was the factory legislation of the 1830's in Britain. In due course came legislation for public health, public schools, food and drug laws, municipal trading, subsidies, embargoes, tariffs, and other "government interference." *The most drastic interference, however, did not come from the government at all, but from the trusts, monopolies, and trade associations of the businessman, and from the labor unions of the workers.*

The guardians of the market theory roared their disapproval, but the reaction continued with little interruption down to the crowning debacle when Britain went off gold in 1931. The guardians steadily claimed it all a plot of the radicals. Polanyi reduces this charge to nonsense. He gives a specific account of the tories, aristocrats, statesmen (such as Disraeli, Chamberlain, Bismarck), the tycoons, even the "economic liberals" who championed these assaults upon the Market. The attack followed a similar pattern in all countries, whether they were democracies, constitutional monarchies, or despotisms.

Something very deep and very powerful was obviously at work. To fit this historical development into the theory of the class struggle, into fights between radicals and reactionaries, or into standard theories of property, is impossible. The facts come running out of all the cracks. But they fit easily into a flesh-and-blood social structure spontaneously trying to protect itself against the ravages of a cold mathematical Market. For example, according to market philosophy nothing must be undertaken unless it "pays." Unemployed persons can rot by the thousands if it does not pay some enterpriser to hire them. Clearly no society can long tolerate such a destructive taboo. It is worse than foot-binding or child marriage. It is a form of human sacrifice.

The monopoly movement thus appears in a strange new light, as a natural human defense. Monopolies were formed to protect businessmen from the violent ups and downs of the Market, precisely as trade unions were developed to protect workers from the howling blizzards of the free market in labor. If monopolies are part of this social defense mechanism, clearly they cannot be liquidated blindly. If they are broken up in a flood of cease and desist orders, they will surely form again as soon as the government lawyers go home to get a little sleep.

I do not know whether Polanyi's thesis will finally stand the test of history, but it accounts for most of the facts, without moral judgments against individuals. If the Market was destructive to that vague but powerful entity which we call society, then it followed naturally that we should have government interference, labor unions, and business monopolies — Big Business, Big Unions, Big Government.

Keep the Machines Running

What is the fundamental trouble with monopoly? On Polanyi's showing, it is not greed, or even arbitrary power, though both are often in the picture. The real trouble is a negative thing: *restriction of output,* holding down, holding back, holding up the flow of goods. A monopoly, whether of business, labor or other producers' group, is constantly seeking that level of output which will best protect its members — usually for the short run.[7]

Animated by fear of loss, once their vested interests are built up, monopolists often become timid. They are afraid of new ideas and inventions — to lock 'em up is safer. They are the antithesis of the venture capital man who was always ready to risk his last dollar to make a million.

"For every individual and for the community," observes C. E. Ayres, "the criterion of value is the continuation of the life process — keeping the machines running. That is what we have in fact been doing throughout the ages, and that is what we must continue to do better — if we are to exceed the achievements of the past."[8]

Dilemma

To the extent that monopolies do keep the machines from running, they tend to reduce the investment of savings in productive enterprise and aggravate the problem of idle money. They could limit employment even if the dollar circuit were closed. A government trying to underwrite full employment on the principle of a compensatory economy, as outlined in the preceding book in this series,[9] might never be able to close the circuit as fast as the monopolists broke it open.

On the other hand, the flight to monopolistic methods might not be so urgent when compensatory devices were operating to begin with. If Polanyi is right, monopolies have been formed

7. The "deadly formula" of high unit prices, described in Chapter 2, is an illustration of this.
8. *The Theory of Economic Progress,* University of North Carolina Press, 1944.
9. *Where's the Money Coming From?,* The Twentieth Century Fund, 1943.

more for defense than for offense. It is a nice question how far monopolists would go in restricting production if there were no business cycle.

This is pretty theoretical, however. Actually we have a number of great monopolies, or near-monopolies, practicing a businesslike restriction of output, and filling the price structure with inflexible elements — like sulphur at $18 a ton, year in, year out. They have expert lobbies at Washington and in the state capitols to fortify their position. Actually if the President and Congress, after the war, set up compensatory machinery to maintain full employment, the monkey wrenches of the monopolists might well throw it completely out of gear.

Are They Inevitable?

In Chapter 11 we will outline a program for the control of monopolies. It is a bare outline, for Americans have not got down to brass tacks on the question. Monopolies have been considered primarily in moral terms. We are not going to get far until we consider them in more objective terms. Some monopolies are "good," some are "bad," some are certainly inevitable — and every one is different. Each needs to be judged on its merits, and the chief criterion is whether this particular outfit helps to keep the machines running.

Assuming that certain monopolies do slow up the machines, and must be brought under the control of the community, is the community strong enough to do it? Who's in charge around here anyway, in the mid-1940's? Many liberals believe that big business has been in charge, is now in charge during the war, and will continue in charge after the war. I doubt if the situation is quite as simple as this. The liberals are using class struggle dialectics on a world where such mental calipers are out of date.

Rope Trick

Big business — and I am thinking now specifically of top management in the one hundred great companies which have 70 per cent of war orders — is exceedingly powerful in some respects. But as a substitute for the accredited government, neither its credentials nor its prospects are too good, in my opinion. Among other reasons are these:

1. The gentlemen do not want to assume the duties and responsibilities of government. That has not been part of their training. Which one of them is ready to guarantee 57,000,000 jobs, or draw the blueprints for averting World War III?

2. Their interests are diverse, as we noted in our review of business pressure groups. They have a united front in such ideological matters as the virtues of private enterprise, but they lack a united front in practical matters — such as who is going to get the cream of the passenger traffic after the war — airways, railways, or highways?

3. They are increasingly vulnerable in an interdependent high-energy society. In a depression, most of them go down with the rest of us, no matter how high they maintain their prices, or how tight their control of output.

4. Finally, they live in a kind of judicial vacuum, because in many cases the managers of our great corporations have deprived stockholders of all de facto control of their property. Thus, as Peter Drucker has emphasized, they have cut the nexus with property which makes their position secure and legitimate.[10] They represent no interest but themselves, a small, self-perpetuating class, the crowning triumph of nightwork in the offices of corporation lawyers.

10. *The Future of Industrial Man,* John Day, 1942.

The result has been a disorderly industrial scramble in which the public interest is largely neglected. The managers have had power without responsibility. The plantation owners in the South before the Civil War, the lords of the manor in medieval Europe, did better than that; they were tyrants, but they accepted responsibility for their people, and for the land.[11]

Sooner or later a showdown must come as to whether the managers of big business and big monopoly are to run the community or the community is to run them. When it does come, we may find that big business is perched way up in the sky by a kind of Indian rope trick. It might fall down pretty fast.

11. Some of our businessmen, as we shall see later, are beginning to think about their responsibilities.

7

LABOR PRESSURES

Workers too have broken out of the free market where labor is a commodity. They have organized monopolies and near monopolies like farmers and businessmen. They have fixed their prices which are wages, and restricted output by means of collective bargaining and the closed shop. Much of the discussion in the preceding chapters can be applied to labor groups as well as to management groups.

Far more citizens are of course involved, though we cannot make a direct comparison because of the difficulty of estimating the "business" population as distinguished from people employed by business. We know that the managers who make the ultimate business decisions are a relatively small group.

There are today about 65,000,000 Americans at work. Twelve million of them are in the armed services, 53,000,000 in wage and salary jobs, and in the ranks of the self-employed — like farmers, shopkeepers and your author. Perhaps 10,000,000 are thus not eligible for unions. That leaves 43,000,000. Of this number about 30 per cent belong to labor organizations, as follows:

In the AF of L	6,000,000
In the CIO	5,000,000

In the United Mineworkers	600,000
In the railroad brotherhoods and other "independents"	1,000,000
Total	12,600,000

Thus the workers of America are far from being completely organized, especially in retail and wholesale establishments, in selling, finance and the service trades generally. Heavy industry is now pretty well organized. Never was "labor" so strong in membership, power and funds, yet seldom has it been in a more precarious position.

Strikes in Wartime

As I write, the Philadelphia streetcar strike is drawing to a close, with its leaders in jail and the Army protecting the traffic. The fact that the strike was the direct result of fear that Negroes would get white men's jobs in the critical postwar period hardly came to the surface at all. The fact that the strike did slow down war production was on everybody's tongue. Some Negroes were upgraded and the men went out in terror of the future. If they had been sure of keeping their jobs they might have agreed to the upgrading, and kept at work. The public, without understanding all this, remembers the coal strikes of 1943, and the threatened railway strike. The temper of the public is ugly, and rising.

Unions are at the moment even more unpopular than Congressmen. Their members and leaders should face the fact that they are not living in a community at peace. In a community engaged in total war, a strike of war workers, or those who supply war workers, is in effect a strike against the community, not against the bosses. Nothing could be more disastrous to the labor movement. It is made all the worse by the solemn pledges of both the AF of L and the CIO to refrain from strikes for the duration. Man-days lost through strikes are far lower since Pearl Harbor, but one man-day lost in war enrages the public more than a hundred man-days lost in peace. The criterion has changed.

Public Polls

Recent polls of public opinion show overwhelming majorities against strikes, and a rapidly growing resentment against unions in general. In Germany, before Hitler, the unions were experienced, powerful, with more members relatively than in this country. Yet they disappeared almost overnight.[1] Their members did not have a cause for which to fight; at least they did not fight. Unions went down and out with the same finality that big business went down and out — the Thyssens and the Krupps.

Here are the results of a *Fortune* poll covering tests of the whole population in February 1944:

	Percentage agreeing
Labor unions have done an excellent job and should be given more power	7
Labor unions have made mistakes, but they have done more good than harm and should be supported	28
Labor unions have done some good in the past, but they have gone too far and should be curbed by law	49
Labor unions should be abolished	7
Don't know	9
Total	100

1. See Adolf Sturmthal, *The Tragedy of European Labor, 1918–1939,* Columbia University Press, 1943.

This is a public reaction to throw the fear of God into any leader of labor. When the Connally-Smith bill to curb unions was before Congress, a Gallup poll showed 67 per cent of the nation for it, only 24 per cent against it, and 9 per cent undecided. The record since its passage proves that it was a thoroughly stupid act. It was not, however, judged by the public on its technical merits; it was judged on its apparent ability to make strikes illegal in wartime. Meanwhile men in the Army break into unprintable profanity at the thought of having their weapons held up.

The AF of L

The American Federation of Labor was organized in 1886 about the time when "trusts" were forming in one industry after another. The class struggle was prominently mentioned by the AF of L in the preamble to its original constitution, and never heard from again. The Knights of Labor in the 1870's had had a good deal to say about crusading for a better world. The AF of L, however, hewed to the line of getting more cash for the membership, and supporting the candidates of any political party who would further this practical aim.

World War I brought the unions out of the basement. Samuel Gompers took his seat at high councils along with Bernard Baruch. By 1920, there were four million workers in the AF of L, organized largely in craft unions. During the prosperous '20's the membership declined. By 1933, at the bottom of the depression, it had fallen to 2,126,000.

The CIO

With the New Deal Administration and partial recovery, union membership began to climb again. In 1935, John L. Lewis took his United Mine Workers, a vertical industrial union containing all crafts, out of the AF of L, and founded the CIO. It was pledged to the promotion of more vertical industrial unions, and proceeded to make life miserable for big business in steel, rubber, automobiles, aircraft and elsewhere. (Lewis has since walked his miners out of the CIO.)

In the same year, Congress passed the Wagner Act, often called a Magna Carta for labor. This act made it easy to organize workers, where before it had always been hard, and in some areas, as much as one's life was worth. The Wagner Act required management to bargain collectively when a union representing the majority of the workers should demand it. For management to interfere with the organization of workers became an illegal act.

This greatly stimulated the young CIO. It grew like a weed until it was as large as the AF of L — which was also growing under the fertilization of the Wagner Act. The CIO grew large and strong but it also became unpopular. Its sit-down strikes made labor history, but infuriated many middle-class people because of the violation of accepted ideas about property. It is a curious thing that businessmen, on the firing line, accepted the new unions on the whole with less resentment than did the farmers and white-collar classes.

If World War I took labor leaders out of the cellar, World War II put them in the front parlor. Sidney Hillman of the Amalgamated Clothing Workers, affiliated with the CIO, was made associate director, a kind of joint czar, along with William Knudsen, over the first edition of the War Production Board. In theory, labor was an equal partner with industry.

Labor Lobbies

Meanwhile the AF of L, the CIO and the railway brotherhoods are in pressure group politics up to their necks. W. M.

Kiplinger notes that the unions own more fancy real estate in Washington than any other pressure group, and estimates that their various marble palaces cost ten million dollars.[2] The CIO, according to Mr. Kiplinger, is still pretty green at the game of lobbying; the AF of L puts on a more finished performance. They often line up together to fight antistrike legislation, using much the same methods as the business and farm groups, on the time-honored principle of Me First. This causes considerable distress to their liberal friends, who like to think of "labor" as a company of Galahads.

The labor lobby was virtually Sam Gompers' creation. Yet he would be profoundly shocked, if he could come up from those nether regions to which our best people consigned him, to observe the way the unions lean on government today. Our best people might change their minds and get up a dinner for Sam at the Waldorf.

As compared with any particular business lobby, the labor lobby serves more people, and people who often need that service very bitterly. The history of the miners, studied fairly, is full of hardship, poverty, injustice and brutal repression. They were a commodity to be dealt in, like the coal they hacked from the seams. The power that Lewis has won for them now, in a sense, offsets the power that the operators have had for many years. Big Union has caught up with Big Business, and in that there is a kind of rough justice. But neither side has found its just place in the whole community. The fact that the miners are now well enough organized to freeze city dwellers, or shut down war industry, or bring the railroads to a standstill is no great satisfaction to the rest of us.

2. *Washington Is Like That*, Harper, 1942.

Labor Restricts Output

James Caesar Petrillo, head of the American Federation of Musicians, an AF of L union, is the man who says whether or not you can play a phonograph record, or listen to a radio transcription. Unless his union is in on the pay-off, you cannot play or listen. Petrillo has repeatedly forbidden worthy noncommercial entertainments which could not afford to pay the tribute. It is the Hartford-Empire all over again. He has defied Congress, the Administration, the courts, and furnished one of the prize examples of Me First in organized labor. The *St. Louis Post Dispatch* is a great liberal newspaper, forever fighting the battles of the common man. On July 1, 1944 it had this to say editorially about James Caesar Petrillo:

It seems probable that the only efficacious way of handling Petrillo is by frontal attack, and by frontal attack he shall assuredly be handled. He is conducting a strike; he is attempting a monopoly. He is restraining interstate commerce. Those circumstances should enable the law of the land to deal with him with the bluntness he has earned.

Thurman Arnold, who certainly did not start out with an anti-labor bias, has made out a bill of particulars against some unions which is as full of red pepper as his bills against various business monopolies.[3] Both, of course, come out of his experience in trying to enforce the Sherman Act. He makes the following specific charges against certain labor organizations, especially in the building trades:

They lobby for price-fixing — as in the case of plumbing supplies.
They try to eliminate low-cost methods of distribution which would aid the consumer.
They create local trade barriers by restricting the use of materials produced outside a given state.

3. *Cosmopolitan Magazine,* November 1943.

They block the entrance of new firms into the field — in cahoots with their employers.

They are bitterly opposed to laborsaving devices.

They try to put legal limits on the amount of work a man can do.

In certain cases, they try to make employers pay for no work at all. This is a similar objective to that of the AAA, where farmers were paid for *not* raising things.

Feather Beds

The government plowed under cotton — or had the farmers do it — to boost the price and help the cotton farmers. The aluminum monopoly, according to *Fortune,* plows under new inventions for making the metal from common clays. The unions, some of them, plow under good materials, and good man-hours, by such practices as these, popularly known as feather bedding:

Painters' unions in various cities will not permit the use of spray guns, which save time and paint. Even in war they are afraid of the bad example which might be set. (The "thin-entering-wedge" argument.)

A local in the teamsters' union requires that every truck entering the New York metropolitan area have a local driver in addition to the driver already employed.

In Chicago, employers cannot bring in cement mixers mounted on trucks unless they hire extra men to stand around and watch.

In many theatres a "full crew" of scene shifters must be employed, even in plays where the scenery is not changed at all.

In some cases the plumbing unions will install pipes made to measure in the factory only if the thread at one end is removed and a new thread cut at the job site.

Doubtless it is unjust that the public takes quite calmly the monopolistic practices of Hartford-Empire in the field of glass bottles, but gets all burned up by union feather-bed practices. But that is the way the public feels. It would be the course of wisdom if the labor leaders involved in these practices would figure up sometime how much they stand to lose in the long view. Businessmen are not going to run unions out of town; they have too much in common. If the time ever comes, soldiers are more likely to do it, with the middle class behind them.

If I were a labor leader today I should tread very gently. I would not fight for feather beds or for special privileges, or try to double-rivet any monopolies I might have. I would retire James Caesar Petrillo in jig time to the kettledrums, or wherever he came from. I would, however, fight until I dropped for decent working conditions, for health and safety measures, and especially for a national plan for full employment after the war.

Re-establishing Diplomatic Relations

Some of the younger leaders have noticed the way the wind is blowing. Here, for instance, is the United Steelworkers Union, CIO, the second largest in the country, with 726,000 members. The officers called in a firm of C.P.A.'s to go over the books, and then they published the report to the world. That was one of the wisest things a union ever did. It re-established diplomatic relations with the public.

Here is R. J. Thomas, president of the biggest union — the Automobile Workers, CIO, with more than a million members. A wave of wildcat strikes had broken over Detroit in the spring of 1944. They froze Mr. Thomas' blood. He roared at his members: "If you value your union, if you want to see it live . . . we must restrain ourselves and our hot-headed brothers today. If we do not, there will be no union after the war."

The unions cannot go it alone any more than big business. Their future lies in serving the community interest as well as their shop interests. The community can break them if it comes to a showdown. J. Raymond Walsh of the research department of the CIO has stated the case well:[4]

I believe the greatest single object of organized labor should be graduation from the purely pressure-group approach to problems of hours and wages, prices and working conditions, to one of national leadership in the welfare of this country. The day of the self-interest pressure group is past. Instead, this is a time when no group can be secure in an insecure society; a time when the pragmatist works for the security of his fellow men in order to secure his own.

In the last sentence, Mr. Walsh has given the theme of this book.

4. *Antioch Review*, Summer 1943.

8

LABOR BOSSES

THE SCENE is the directors' room of a well-known company in New Jersey. The directors have done themselves well, with high ceilings, windows to the floor, and cream-colored walls as a background for oil portraits of officers of the company. The face of one past officer you would all recognize.

Ten men are conferring around a big T-shaped table. At first glance they seem to be all of one type. All are well dressed, all speak easily and well, as if they were used to being listened to without interruption. The expression on most of the faces is pleasant, but touched with that tense worry which is so common where men produce things in America.

Is this the fortnightly meeting of the board of directors? It is not. It is a meeting of the labor-management committee of the company, set up at the request of the War Production Board. I have come to write a story about it for a magazine. Standing there on the soft carpet beside the green baize table, I cannot tell who are the managers and who are the labor members! I suddenly realize how rapidly class lines are melting in America. I think of my daughter, going from college to overalls in an airplane factory. Who is "labor" and who is "capital"?

Managers All

The men around the table look alike and talk alike because they act alike. They are all of them managers of large, complicated organizations. Let us listen to Will Herberg, himself a union man, describe why this is so and how it has come about.[1] It is something that few students of the class struggle have yet caught up with.

The rank-and-file union member, says Mr. Herberg, frequently enjoys less freedom in relation to his own union leadership than in relation to his employer. He has more protection against arbitrary power exerted by his employer than by his union officials. He is often under very severe penalties for exercising ordinary civil "rights" in his union, such as organizing minority parties, issuing leaflets, holding meetings, denouncing officials. He can damn the President of the United States until he is black in the face, but he had better keep his mouth shut about Mr. Big in his union front office. "The effective power of top officials is greater, their grip tighter, their tenure more secure, their conduct less open to criticism and control, than is commonly the case in our federal or state governments in normal times."

These are facts of ordinary experience which only special pleading can deny. Yet the trade-union movement is fundamentally a democratic one, born of the need to protect people from being bought and sold like bags of cement. Why this paradox? Because, says Mr. Herberg, a union today has a dual nature. *First,* it is a business-like service organization operating many complicated situations, which require highly expert technical handling. *Second,* it is a vehicle of the historic movement of the workers for social recognition and democratic self-determination.

1. *Antioch Review,* Fall 1943.

The first function requires bureaucratic efficiency, as in the case of a big bank or insurance company. The members are clients entitled to the best service for their money. They should *not* interfere with the management. The second requires, however, that the rank and file have complete freedom of expression, and maintain control over general policy.

"The union, as an institution, is thus in the grip of a very real contradiction." The situation often gives conscientious leaders a "psychic cleavage," trying to look two ways at once. In the early days the democratic function is usually dominant. But as the union consolidates its position, and enters into complicated negotiations with management, the business-service function comes to the fore.

"The Office"

In the beginning, the town-meeting procedure is followed, with an executive board elected from the floor, and the only official a recording secretary. Gradually these democratic habits fade out. The officials devote all their time to union affairs, are paid larger and larger salaries, until finally they become "The Office," a self-perpetuating managing group.

All power in the union, administrative, legislative and judicial, is concentrated in The Office, which becomes highly skilled in the technicalities of collective bargaining. Salaries range up to five figures. In some unions, Mr. Big never retires until they carry him out feet first. There are some AF of L union leaders who have been there as long as I can remember, and I am no longer young.

"The tendency toward the concentration of power is inherent in the very nature of the organization. As it grows, its functions multiply and its responsibilities increase." Mr. Herberg believes that the thirst for power is secondary. Even the most idealistic administrators become career men because of their technical tasks. To draw up a wage-rate schedule for an industry, for instance, often calls for setting thousands of different rates, each requiring special knowledge.

"What Are They Getting Paid For?"

In short, a large national union is trapped in the type of bureaucratic difficulties which beset every large organization, be it business, university, church or government. Union members become like stockholders in great companies, content so long as they get their "dividends," i.e., favorable contracts with their employers. As in the case of corporations — and governments too — the administration is constantly calling on the members (stockholders, citizens) to "be more active," to "take an interest"; but the call is pure formality. The administrators would be terrified if the members actually did become active. Indeed there is little for union members to be active about, for The Office does it all for them.

Union elections are as empty and meaningless as in the case of most large corporations. One has a proxy, called a ballot, and a wastebasket. He can use the ballot to vote for an administration stooge, or he can use the wastebasket to throw the ballot in. Says the average member: "Let the officials run the union; that's what they are getting paid for." As long as things go well he does not want self-government. He is annoyed and resentful when attempts are made to force responsibilities upon him. What he wants is "service and protection, his money's worth for his dues." In a similar psychological condition, the stockholder wants his conventional dividend and no responsibility for operating his "property." "What's the management paid for?"

Mr. Herberg's story runs parallel to James Burnham's thesis in

The Managerial Revolution, though he is far more specific than is Mr. Burnham. George Soule reaches a similar conclusion when he says: "The usual union leader becomes a skilled politician, devoted to keeping power, protecting vested rights, and advancing a little today and tomorrow — enough to prove his usefulness to his constituents, but not enough to upset the environment in which he operates."[2] These facts, continues Mr. Soule, are somewhat obscured in the public mind by the revolutionary language and the ideology which the labor leader has inherited from an earlier day.

You can now realize why I had trouble in that New Jersey plant telling who was worker and who employer. They are all really in the same line of business. They are The Office, the managers, the powerhouse. One group has stockholders to keep happy, the other union members. So their behavior, their very faces, take on a common type.

It is interesting to observe this relation working out in the case of John L. Lewis, and the 600,000 men of the United Mine Workers Union. When Lewis defied the President in 1943 and ordered a coal strike, the miners followed him almost to a man. They trusted him because they had no one else to trust. He had fought their battles and got results, time after time. They were not critical of his methods; indeed they admired the way he outwitted the forces they believed were arrayed against them. If he said he had been double-crossed by Washington, that meant more to them than all the newspaper editorials, all the radio blasts, the speeches by Congressmen and prominent citizens. One miner put it this way: "We pay John L. Lewis $25,000 a year to look after us. He's doing that and we'll go right on doing what he says."[3]

2. *Foreign Affairs,* April 1944.
3. Craig Thompson in *The New York Times,* May 10, 1943.

Unions as a Function of Business

Unions in America are not anticapitalist. In one sense they are a function of the business system. If there were no businessmen there would be no unions — fundamentally it is as simple as that. If private enterprise should vanish, the power of the unions would vanish too — as it did in Russia. Otherwise the role of labor would be to fight the government, which, as Euclid used to say, is absurd. Unions battle with management over the division of the receipts which they jointly earn, but there is nothing revolutionary about that. No American union thinks that labor earns it all. No union — except possibly the IWW — ever aimed at the dictatorship of the proletariat. It is safe to say no union ever will, after the demonstration of what happened to unions in Russia.

Barbara Ward finds a similar situation in Britain.[4] In recent years, she says, trade-union leaders and employers have been working hand in glove to obtain a "closed corporate structure" within which high prices and reduced output can be won at the expense of the consumer. This is economic pressure rather than political, and more successful than the Labor Party. The young men in the armed forces, "where the practical get-the-job-done approach is strongest, and the sense of class relationships weakest," look on the Labor Party as irrelevant. The Party intones a rigid formula invented in the 19th century and since unchanged. It bores the youngsters worse than learning dead languages. The reformers have not cleared up anything by trying to interpret the 20th century world in Marxian terms. "Labor monopolies," says Miss Ward, leveling a good part of the Marxian structure in one sentence, "do not break capitalist monopolies, they join them."

In this way they exert artificial pressure on price levels, and compound the damage done by business monopolies.

4. *The New Republic,* October 26, 1942.

Labor When Peace Comes

Strong as the unions are now, they face a critical situation if and when peace brings a bad depression.[5] Full employment, like the guaranteed profits of war industries, is not an automatic proposition. Let the national income fall below $100 billion and see how unions look. On the whole, organized labor would probably fall faster and harder than organized business. Its cash reserves are less, and its bosses have more members to placate.

Take the Kaiser shipyards in Portland, Oregon, as an example of what labor is up against when the war ends. We know that whatever they may make in these shipyards it will not be many ships. The company, the Portland Chamber of Commerce, and the U. S. Maritime Commission sponsored a joint survey in early 1944 of the 81,881 workers in the plant. Almost two thirds of them, it was found, came from *outside* Portland, and almost half of these intended to go on living in Portland after the war. Yet 86 per cent of the whole force, 70,000-odd workers, *had no postwar job in sight except with Kaiser!* Can you imagine the stampede when the men realize that there are no more ships to build? How can the union handle any such mass problem as this? What happens to wage rates, to dues, to the union treasury, to the big shots in The Office?

Threefold Disadvantage

In May 1944, the Senate Military Affairs Committee, in the person of Senator Murray of Montana, estimated nineteen million unemployed immediately after the close of the war, and called for legislation to control the reconversion to peace.[6] Can

5. Some economists expect an inflationary boom with depression later. I do not, but I may be wrong.
6. *The New York Times,* May 13, 1944.

union structures hold together in the face of such a torrent? The London *Economist,* somewhat smugly perhaps, has indicated the pickle that not only the labor movement, but the whole country, is likely to be in:[7]

It is impossible to feel very happy about the prospects of full employment in the United States. He would be a rash man who would prophesy with absolute assurance that it will be attained in Great Britain. But America is at a three-fold disadvantage as compared to Britain. First, the American problem is far greater: the output of the American economy is now more than 50 percent higher than in any peacetime year, which means that the total of civilian demand will have to be increased by roughly half, and then kept at this figure if there is not to be mass unemployment. Secondly, there is a substantial theoretical and practical agreement in Britain on the methods to be pursued in maintaining the volume of effective demand; in America, all is still controversy. And thirdly, there is an accepted administrative machine in Britain to carry the policy out; in America, the machinery in so far as it exists at all, is the object of violent political attack. [Meaning the attack on the "bureaucrats."]

Just to make everything lovely, the evidence is accumulating of large increases in output per man-hour due to new inventions, new processes, new methods of training workers. Which means that after the war, the country can achieve a given volume of production with far fewer workers than in 1940. Labor shortages have caused immense pressure to speed up laborsaving devices and methods.[8] Technological unemployment is of course poison to the labor movement.

Westbrook Pegler seems to be lashing himself and foaming at the mouth unnecessarily. The labor movement is not going to take

7. April 15, 1944.
8. Witness the Job Methods Training program of the War Manpower Commission, which gives foremen a capsule course in scientific management.

over the country in the face of this situation. If Big Business is up in the air on one Indian rope trick, Big Unions are up there on another. Neither can go it alone during demobilization, nor can they get far by an offensive and defensive alliance.

What Workers Want

Coming back to the 75 per cent of American workers who are not in the labor movement, Elmo Roper, who does the polls for *Fortune,* has given us an eloquent and accurate picture of what *all* workers want, whether organized or not.[9] As the result of many polls he finds that they want four things, in this order:

First, security. Three times as many workers want an annual guaranteed wage as want labor-management committees; while "steady employment is a paramount consideration to 10 times as many workers as is high pay, and to 25 times as many as short hours." Most workers feel that the federal government should guarantee security in the form of full employment.

Second, a chance to advance. This is in the good old American tradition.

Third, to be treated like human beings. Workers strongly object to being regarded as commodities. This finding supports Polanyi's thesis, developed earlier.

Fourth, to feel important. Workers want to think that they are "personally performing in a job which contributes something to the aggregate of human happiness; that they are working at something worthwhile."

Mr. Roper comes to a wise conclusion. "In describing what labor wants perhaps I have only been describing what everyone, everywhere, wants." Note, however, that he has not described what labor pressure groups are working for.

9. *American Mercury,* February 1944.

The war has made industrial workers out of thousands of middle and upper bracket folk who never used their hands before. It has upgraded manual workers into supervisors, managers, all manner of white-collar tasks. It has taught young men in the services many new skills and professions — for example, 100,000 new airplane pilots have been graduated so far. The war is like a giant concrete mixing machine, shaking the classes together, grinding up class barriers.

What is going to come out of the hopper? In Chapter 11 we will hazard a few guesses.

9

PRESSURE FROM FARMERS

In 1800, four out of five Americans lived on farms. Now only about one out of five lives there, approximately 25 million people. Another 20 per cent of the population live in rural areas, but do no commercial farming. They are storekeepers, mechanics, carpenters, agents, who serve, or live off, the farmer, according to your point of view. Thus fewer than half our people now make their home in the great open spaces. Yet the rural folklore is still strong. The homespun virtues of Calvin Coolidge made him the perfect symbol of leadership. Every morning on its editorial page *The New York Times* (population New York, 8,000,000) celebrates the Old Oaken Bucket.

There are more than six million separate farms, mostly strung along the roads. In Europe farmers tend to live in the village and go out to their fields. Three American farms out of five are occupied by their owners, two by tenants. Tenantry has been increasing very rapidly.

In New England, where dairying predominates, the average size of a farm is 100 acres. In the corn and hog belt of the Middle West it is 160 acres; in the cotton belt, 80; and in the wheat fields of the Great Plains, where the combines wallow like tanks, it is 400 acres.

There are perhaps a million marginal farms where the soil is so thin or so eroded that most years people cannot make a living. They keep afloat on relief, unless the Farm Security Administration can help them find a better piece of land. There is a big increase at both ends of the scale. The practice of "twilight farming," where mill workers come home to tend the garden patch, was increasing even before the war. There is also a growing number of big factory farms, where migratory workers constitute the uncertain labor supply, and farming as a way of life has about disappeared. Since 1930 these big farms of more than 1,000 acres have increased 25 per cent, while little farms of under 50 acres have decreased 15 per cent.[1]

After the collapse of farmland values and crop prices in 1920, following World War I, agriculture remained largely in the dumps all through the prosperous '20's. Prices for most crops were down. In the depression, the situation became revolutionary in some areas. Foreclosures were being halted with shotguns, as farmers took the law into their own hands.

During the '20's they were given crop and mortgage loans on a small scale, a little tariff protection, and a veto by President Coolidge of the McNary-Haugen bill, which proposed helping them more substantially. Under President Hoover they got the Federal Farm Board, which disbursed $500,000,000 to buy surplus crops. This looks generous until one remembers that values at the same time were dropping by the billions.

New Deal for Farmers

In 1933 the new Administration began giving farmers many

1. Figures in above paragraphs from Evans Clark, *Wartime Facts and Postwar Problems,* The Twentieth Century Fund, 1943.

of the things they had long been clamoring for: higher prices, cheaper credit, subsidies, mortgage relief. Most farmers were mighty glad to get this help after thirteen lean years, three of them altogether dreadful.

To give the farmers so many of the things they wanted, the New Deal had to increase central planning. In effect it organized agriculture as one stupendous business, with headquarters in Washington, and Henry Wallace in charge. By a curious irony the individualistic, freedom-loving, leave-me-alone farmers of the nation were the first major group to become integrated in an over-all national plan. Furthermore, their own organizations helped to draft the plan. The banks, the railroads, the insurance companies, the unemployed, received cash relief; but agriculture was in ef-fect collectivized — lifted clean out of the free market and put in a market where prices, or production, or both, were controlled. If this seems a strong statement, look at the following record:

1. The AAA removed cotton, corn, rice, tobacco, wheat — the great staples — from the free market. The resulting control was comparatively democratic. Farmers first voted whether they wanted it, and then after the majority had voted yes — as they mostly did — the farmers themselves, in 2500 local county boards, administered the Act.

The AAA procedure was roughly as follows. Experts in the Department of Agriculture figured out how much of a crop could be sold at prices to satisfy the farmer — say 12 million bales of cotton. Then they prorated the total to each cotton-growing state, where it was prorated to each cotton-growing county, where the local board prorated it to each cotton-growing farm. If the farmer held to his allotment, he was paid in Treasury checks for not growing more. When the Supreme Court declared this unconsti-tutional, the farmer was paid for taking conservation measures, improving his soil, rotating cover crops — which had the same effect of holding his cotton acreage to the allotted figure.

If exceptionally fine weather brought a bigger crop than estimated, the government took over the surplus, giving the farmer cash and taking the crop as security. If nature, on the other hand, was unfair to organized farmers, the government insured the farmer against loss. This did not apply to all crops, but to some of the big staples.

2. For crops which the AAA did not cover, the Food Stamp Plan bought up the surplus and held the price at levels satisfactory to the farmers.

3. Butter surpluses were purchased by a special government corporation, and warehoused in cold storage to maintain prices.

4. Various "marketing agreements" were entered into. Take milk, for instance. The milk marketing agreement amounted to a government-sponsored monopoly in which dairy farmers, creameries, distributors to doorsteps, united to control production and maintain prices in the New York milk shed, or the Chicago milk shed.

5. For poor farmers the Farm Security Administration was established, to make them loans for seeds, fertilizer, tools, a mule, a house, and to put them on their feet again. A million were so helped.

6. A series of vast government credit agencies lent farmers billions of dollars at low rates of interest for first mortgages, second mortgages, crop loans, market loans, processing loans, cooperative loans. The government saved hundreds of thousands of farms from foreclosure in the depression.

7. The Department of Agriculture went after the middleman with a number of severe statutes. It also had some very mean surprises for speculators in agricultural commodities.

8. The Rural Electrification Administration brought electric power to more than a million farms.

Married to Government

The above is not a complete list, but it is enough, I think, to warrant Mr. Kiplinger's statement that "Farmers as a class have gotten themselves married to government and there is no possibility of divorce or separation."[2] It warrants the conclusion of two Pennsylvania dirt farmers: "If the government should step out of the picture today, American farming would collapse,"[3] and the remark of a Washington correspondent in 1940: "Once the farm organizations stand united they can get anything out of Congress short of good growing weather."[4]

This record also lends support to Dr. Polanyi's thesis, described in Chapter 6. He concluded, you will remember, that neither "labor" nor "land" could remain indefinitely as a mere commodity on the automatic Market. Society would revolt against it. Certainly American agriculture has revolted in a big way since 1933, with crop after crop taken out of the free market to be managed collectively. It is interesting to note that this historical drive was paralleled by another one taking "labor" out of the free market via the Wagner Act, the Wages and Hours law, the National Labor Board, and a great increase in the area of collective bargaining.

Can six million farmers be thrown back on their own resources when the war ends? Only in after dinner speeches and campaign oratory. The farmers are married to the government and there are no divorce laws in this court. When farm prices start

2. W. M. Kiplinger, *Washington Is Like That,* Harper, 1942.
3. P. Alston Waring and Walter Magnes Teller, *Roots in the Earth,* Harper, 1943. The best book on American farming I have ever read.
4. Kenneth Crawford, *The Pressure Boys,* Julian Messner, 1939.

slipping after this war, as they did after World War I, the marriage knot will pull the tighter. Furthermore the Farm Bloc has blessed the union.

The Farm Bloc

The business bloc started with the tariff, before 1800. The labor bloc started soon after the trusts, about 1900. The farm bloc in its present phase started with tractors in the 1920's; tractors encourage large-scale commercial farming. It became great and powerful after 1933. Some observers, such as Mr. Kiplinger, think it the smartest, best turned-out lobby in Washington. It controls at least fifteen million votes, "once the organizations stand united."

The "farm bloc" is a loose term covering at least three kinds of members: (1) Congressmen especially amenable to farm legislation; (2) general organizations theoretically representing all kinds of farmers, with their own Washington lobbies; (3) special crop organizations such as the American Livestock Association. This group goes whooping to town whenever it catches the whiff of Argentinian beef. There are three general organizations which count: the Grange, the Farmers Union, and the Farm Bureau Federation.

The Grange was born in 1867 and began lobbying for state railroad regulation almost at once. It helped establish the Interstate Commerce Commission. After that it tended to lapse into local good works, such as oyster suppers for those who could grow the largest pumpkins. It has 800,000 members and a vital part in rural life. But at present its political activity is minor, its leaders timid, worried and very conservative.

The Farmers Union is a progressive outfit of 92,000 members, who fight to help sharecroppers, to retain the Farm Security Administration, and who even join hands with the labor unions occasionally. Its function has been chiefly that of a gadfly, but it may have a considerable future. Its leaders know that the 19th century has gone.

Dreams of Empire

The Farm Bureau Federation is the big shot, the NAM of agriculture. It is administered by a genial southerner named Ed O'Neal, who can make more Congressmen run faster than any man alive. The Federation came in with the tractors after the last war, and represents principally the big commercial farmers, who hire a lot of labor and who are interested in the land more as a source of profit than as a way of life. It claims 690,000 members, and thus must include many family-size farms as well as the hacienda boys.

One of its major goals was to achieve something called "parity." Bassett Jones has labeled parity a hermaphrodite statistical monster. It is based on the average prices farmers got for their crops from 1910 to 1914, when the crop pattern was very different, grades were often different, world conditions far different. It is obvious that "parity" and the free market have nothing in common, for it is a straight price-fixing program.

The Farm Bureau also favors cooperative marketing, when the cooperative is large enough to exercise a bit of monopoly. It favors conservation within reason, and tax reform. It helped draw the teeth of the Copeland pure food and drug bill. It almost killed the Administration's war subsidy program, because the Farm Bureau chiefs felt the program held down agricultural prices.

The Farm Bureau is tied up in a direct way with the Department of Agriculture. Some of its local representatives hold appointments as government County Agents — which raises the interesting question whether a lobby should be paid by the government to bring pressure on the government. Sometimes the Bureau dictates department policy. It would like to control the department completely, and is in a fair way to do so. It will take a man as tough as Henry Wallace to stand up against Ed O'Neal. The Bureau wants to plow under the small farmer, and the FSA which helps him, so that the big boys may have an abundant supply of cheap farm labor. This repeats on a larger scale the policy of the Associated Farmers of California, who apparently will not be satisfied until they can buy migratory workers on the hoof. Read *The Grapes of Wrath*.

The Farm Bureau neglects, when it does not oppose, farm laborers, little farmers and consumers. It is keen on interfering with the "law" of supply and demand when prices are down, but calls it an irrevocable process of nature when prices are up. Its strongest branches are in the South and Middle West, and it is trying to create a cotton and corn belt coalition to control the House to perpetuity. "As matters now stand," says *Fortune,* "few things in politics are as certain as Ed O'Neal's ability to get votes. . . . On the floor of the House the Farm Bureau can pass or stop *any* farm measure on which it makes a determined fight."[5] The talented Ed works both sides of the street, Republicans and Democrats. He is not, however, quite so omnipotent in the Senate.

Fortune lists five methods by which the Farm Bureau manipulates Congress:

1. It rewards its friends with re-election. Local Bureau organizations get out the vote.
2. It makes it very unpleasant for Congressmen who oppose its measures.

5. June 1944.

3. It defends Congress against the President, which is duck soup for Congressmen. Ed is a spectacular critic of the "bureaucrats."

4. It offers prominence and publicity to friendly legislators.

5. It is very skillful at logrolling and trading with other pressure groups.

Cotton Cartel

The Farm Bureau sages will thoughtfully take a wisp of hay out of their hair, and tell you they are for liberty, free enterprise, sturdy independence, thrift, early rising, and down with the beef trust and government interference. Then they excuse themselves to rush over to the Capitol to make sure that their trained seals are barking loudly against any tampering with their Cotton Cartel — which is as good an example as the next covering the farm bloc's tangible performance in the field of rugged independence.

The "cotton cartel" came in with the New Deal legislation eleven years ago. Under its provisions the Commodities Credit Corporation must lend cotton growers up to 90 per cent of "parity" on their crops. "If prices go up, growers can reclaim their cotton for private sale. But if prices start downward, an artificial scarcity is created — which soon snaps them back. For eleven years cotton growers have unloaded their surpluses on the U. S. taxpayer, and have used the taxpayer's money to build a firm floor under cotton prices."[6] In early 1944 the CCC held seven million bales in storage. "Textile manufacturers," continues *Time*, "squeezed between artificially higher cotton prices and OPA ceilings on their finished goods, protest that no cartel ever dared to manipulate supply and prices so brazenly."

The Farm Bureau uses all the slogans of rugged individualism as a smoke screen behind which it manipulates some of the

6. *Time,* March 27, 1944.

smoothest monopolies known to man. If any American believes that the New Deal agricultural legislation was the product of dreamers, long-haired professors and agents from Moscow, he is a pretty good dreamer himself. It was the product primarily of local farmers crying to be delivered from free competition. Before you blame them, remember where cotton, wheat and beef were in 1932 — 6 cents a pound, 32 cents a bushel, and $3.20 a hundredweight, respectively.

Little Pigs

For eleven years, Henry Wallace has been branded as the murderer of the "little pigs," which shambles has been perhaps Exhibit A in the indictment of the New Deal. The program was devised, according to Lowell Mellett, at a conference of corn and hog farmers from the midwestern states. The pig killing had the approval of the American Farm Bureau Federation, the National Grange, the National Farmers Union, the Corn Belt Meat Producers, and the Central Cooperative Exchange. The gentlemen have maintained a dignified silence all these years, and allowed Mr. Wallace to take the panning. I say panning rather than blame, for, as far as I can learn, the farm bloc was quite justified in asking for the slaughter. It was absolutely necessary unless farmers were to go flat broke in a year when there was not enough corn to bring in the pig crop.

When the Farm Bureau and other general organizations are not applying enough specific heat in Washington, flying columns of prune growers, raisin, citrus, wool, apple, peanut, potato, sugar growers will execute a giant pincer movement on the Capitol, "usually demanding that the government buy up their surpluses to boost the price."[7]

7. W. M. Kiplinger, *Washington Is Like That*, Harper, 1942.

Heads-We-Win

The farm bloc folks not only want "parity"; they demand a 12 per cent bonus above this. They want 90 per cent of the price guaranteed by government loans. "They want these loans," says *The New York Times,* "on the principle of heads-the-farmer-wins-tails-the-taxpayer-loses; for if the farmers' products go below this 90 per cent, the government is to take the loss; but if they go above, the farmer is to pocket the profit."[8] This principle is on all fours with that of the real-estate bloc: if there is any profit in government housing we take it; if there is any loss, the taxpayer takes it. It is the sign of a nicely blocked government that prices are controlled in the interest of special groups, and on principles which, if applied to all groups, would lead to a complete breakdown of the economy.

It is easy to see, the *Times* continues, why we have a bloc government in Congress. "Each Congressman is elected from a particular state or district. Most of them feel responsible only to the voters of their particular district. They will play a particular local interest against the whole national interest if they think that the voters of their district are greedy or short-sighted enough to approve such action."

The farm bloc, like the other super-blocs, is seldom united for long. Its major cleavage is between big and little farmers. But the dairy versus the oleo interests, the livestock versus the poultry interests, do not train well together. Said the *Dairy Record* in 1941: "The dairy industry must set as its goal the complete extermination of oleomargarine." Even the mighty Farm Bureau stands on two legs which traditionally have never traveled long in the same direction: the cotton planters of the South, Democrats to a man; the big corn farmers of Iowa, black Republicans.

8. In an editorial, September 27, 1942.

Living on Our Capital

Farmers used to account for most of the national income, now in peacetime they account for only 10 per cent of it. More important than the national income, however, they account for 33 per cent of the nation's children. Without youngsters from the farms, cities would lose population rapidly.

Despite the fact that for most of their continental existence Americans have farmed for a living — farmers did not drop below 50 per cent of the population until 1880 — and despite the fact that our folklore is based chiefly on the thrift and independence of rural life, we have not been very good farmers. We have been efficient croppers, but that is something else. An efficient cropper can tear the nutriment out of 160 acres in Ohio, and move on to tear it out of 160 acres in Iowa.

As farmers we have lived on our capital, the land. There were three million square miles of it, and many thought it would last forever. We have taken the life-giving elements out and not put an equivalent back. From farming for a living we turned to farming for a cash crop, with "cotton up to the front door." The price of paying off the mortgage was to take it out of the soil.

It is not a mere coincidence that when good new land was no longer to be had free on the frontier, the woes of the farmers multiplied, and presently they were storming Congress. A stern moralist might let them stew in their own juice. Why should taxpayers bail them out for their misuse of the land? The question is academic. You cannot allow 25 to 30 million citizens, men, women and children, to stew in their own juice without wrecking the stability of our society. We have all been takers, not givers. What the farmers have done to the land is no more than what others have done to the forests, the mineral deposits, the oil pools, fisheries, waters. Can you name any considerable river in the nation which is not an open sewer? We are all guilty. Even if we were not, we had better not get too haughty with our farmers if we want to go on eating.

The Future of Farming

The decline in the farm population, while the output of food has been increasing, shows again the effects of the power age. As new machines and methods have made two blades of grass grow where one grew before, the displaced farmers went into factories and boosted the standard of living by manufacturing things. Along in the 1920's, in this country, industry became so efficient that the number of factory workers began to decline. (They are up again now, filling war orders.) These displaced workers went into the service trades, which by 1930 had more people in them than agriculture and factory work combined.

This is the regular rhythm of the power age,[9] the one sure employment guide in the postwar world. *For the long swing, most of the new civilian jobs will have to be found in the service trades.* The farm population will certainly fall below 20 per cent, the factory population will fall below its ratio of 23 per cent in 1940. "In 1943, with a farm population 10 per cent smaller than in 1918, the nation's farmers produced nearly 50 per cent more food on two per cent fewer acres. . . . In 1950, according to rough estimates of the Bureau of Agricultural Economics, the farmers of the nation could duplicate the 1943 record with a 10 per cent further reduction in both man power and crop land. . . ."[10]

9. See Colin Clark, *The Conditions of Economic Progress,* Macmillan of London, 1940.

10. Howard R. Tolley of the Department of Agriculture, writing in *The Progressive,* August 26, 1944.

Back to the Land?

This accredited rhythm reduces to nonsense all back-to-the-land movements as a solution for mass unemployment. Some of us can go back to the land to raise fresh food for our own tables. We can make our victory gardens permanent if we so desire. But we must not forget that when the war demand for food relaxes, in so far as we raise our own stuff we deprive some regular farmer of a market. Back-to-the-land was all right for veterans after the Civil War. It proved highly unsuccessful after World War I. It would be idiotic after this war, except in carefully selected cases. This will not stop demagogues from yelling for it as a cure for all our demobilization ills.

If we took our present war diet and enriched it with all the lend-lease food now sent abroad, we would not be far from a balanced diet for every American. Yet it has been produced with our present agricultural plant, way short of normal man power. Where is there room for millions of additional farmers? Only in somebody's fervid imagination. For another thing, the veterans will not be qualified. To run a modern self-supporting farm, it has been reliably estimated that a man needs not only all-round skills, but an average capital equipment of $12,000.

As soon as the war ends, furthermore, a flood of new processes will be released to make three blades grow where one grew before — hop pickers, cotton pickers, cylinders of gaseous ammonia which, released into irrigation waters, act as high-speed fertilizer. All sorts of new chemicals, gadgets and devices are ready to spread "agrological unemployment" if we try to crowd more people on the land than an adequate standard of national nutrition requires. The Okies are working in the airplane factories at San Diego and in the shipyards at Portland, earning $79.50 a week. Where will they be when government orders are cut way back for planes and ships? Will the grapes of wrath come to another harvest?

The farm bloc can no more stand off the grapes of wrath than Congress can guarantee good growing weather. It will be as helpless as the business bloc or the labor bloc to save itself alone. A postwar world of full employment is a national matter, which can only be worked out by all Americans pulling together. Yet of all answers to the farm problem, full employment is the most conclusive and the most enduring. When city workers have jobs they buy the farmer's food.

There is no future for American farmers, big or little, in restricted output, high scarcity prices, cotton plowed under, eroding soils, jerking puppet strings in Congress. Their future lies in producing a strong, healthy diet for every last American, while getting some enjoyment out of life themselves, and saving the soil for the oncoming generations.

10

BIG GOVERNMENT

Wɪᴛʜ Cᴏɴɢʀᴇssᴍᴀɴ Dᴏᴀᴋs looking for the high sign as to how he shall vote from Ed O'Neal, from the AF of L man, from the NAM lobbyist — and getting pretty cross-eyed in the process — we have about stopped counting on him to represent the whole community. Who does look out for all of us?

There are two answers: we ourselves, and the President of the United States. Neither is a very good answer — not nearly so good as it should be. As individual citizens most of us are adolescent Americans. Our country has been so vast, so rich in natural resources, that it has never occurred to us until lately that anybody needed to be responsible for keeping it going. It is clear, however, that the more responsibility we accept as individuals, the less needs to be taken by the government. If, for instance, all the 40 million Americans who drive cars should suddenly begin taking heed for the anatomy of their neighbors, think of the decline in traffic cops, judges, courts, public ambulances and hospitals!

The Presidency

As Walter Lippmann has pointed out,[1] the only agency which

1. Column in the *New York Herald Tribune*, December 21, 1943. "With-

officially represents all of us is the Presidency — the President himself and his executive aides, including at present a number of special bureaus. As a matter of fact, the President seems to have been cast in this role by the Founding Fathers. Congressmen were supposed to represent the states and localities. Only the President could look over the heads of the clashing local interests and see the nation, steadily and whole. That, at least, was the theory, and there is something in it. If flesh-and-blood Presidents did not have to devote so much time to trying to get re-elected, there might be even more.

In these days, when pressure groups have turned Congress into a sort of revolving door, the necessity for the executive to represent all of us becomes even more urgent. Is this generally recognized and allowed for? It is not. On the contrary, the executive arm is labeled "bureaucracy," and lives in a perpetual blizzard of criticism. This makes it difficult to get the mail signed, let alone do any intensive representing of the whole community.

Intensive representing we must have, however, if the pressure groups are to be controlled. We must have a watchdog devoted to the interest of all the people. As long as the people do not get together and instruct their hired agents, they depend on volunteers, or on chance. In a way, the President acts as a volunteer when he analyzes a public demand and takes action to satisfy it. Sometimes a Congressional committee, like Senator Truman's, acts voluntarily in the public interest, not in response to a definite mandate, but with wide approval once it has acted. Such an administrative bureau as the late National Resources Planning

out strong national leadership by the President, Congress, though it is elected by the people, soon ceases to represent the nation." It represents organized pressure groups led by professionals. It does not hear from the rank and file who have no professionals to speak for them. Only the President can speak for them, says Mr. Lippmann.

Board was created to assist the President (and presumably Congress as well) in studying the consumer interest. Such a bureau as the Farm Security Administration was created to represent a class of farmers who were not articulate enough to apply much pressure, but who badly needed help.

If it were a question of deciding among petitioners, the President would have little difficulty in balancing the pressure groups. Now, however, it has gone beyond that stage. It has become a matter of curbing power which already is overgrown. Nobody, to my knowledge, has the specific task of curbing that power, or even of planning how to curb it. In the next chapter we will investigate some possible measures along that line.

Inadequate Government Machinery

If the government were so organized as to give legitimate representation to economic interests, the pressure groups could never have grown so strong. But our government is not so organized, as we have repeatedly noted. Today industrial, trade, professional, occupational interests are often more important than the geographical interests which are supposed to limit Congressmen.

This is one reason why many Congressmen consider it their duty to represent economic interests which are strong in their states — so that we talk of "Silver" Senators and "Cotton" Ed Smith. The lobbies of these interests take care that the duty shall not be too painful to the Congressmen. Such representing has to be done, however, with a good deal of indirection, because technically Congress is not supposed to take any action favoring special interests.

The relations of government to business, labor and farmer are intricate beyond description. In earlier chapters we have looked at some of the aspects. There is constant give and take. Does government run business in the WPB or do businessmen run government? Both statements are true in part. Does government run the farms or does the farm bloc run government? In giving labor more power, has government weakened its own position? And by government do we mean Congress, the President, the war control boards, or the great departments? We have to look beneath the high abstraction, "Government," in order to find meaning in this powerhouse of clanking gears.

Agenda of the State

What will be the proper functions of our government after the war? A great controversy has been stirred up, in large part by pressure groups, about how much authority the government is to have once peace arrives. To listen to some of the attacks on government activities, one would think public servants were usurping power when they performed the smallest task.

Yet since the first human societies met in caves, there has been a division of labor. Individuals have been responsible for some tasks, and the headman, the elders, the "government" of the tribe, have been responsible for other tasks — especially for the police power, the food supply, justice and military defense. The American government, despite the contempt in which it is widely held, has followed this timeless pattern. It too has been responsible for the police power, military defense, the courts, and since 1933 for the food supply.

Jeremy Bentham, one of the classical political economists, was an uncompromising opponent of government interference. He coined a concept, however, which is still useful after a century. What, he asked, are the Agenda of the State? By this he meant the irreducible minimum of things the government must do to maintain a vital community. And what are the Non-Agenda, the things individuals and private enterprise should do?

Some twenty years ago, John Maynard Keynes, having seen his *Economic Consequences of the Peace* amply vindicated, scanned the heavens and realized that laissez faire as a self-generating system had run its course. That left a serious gap in the economy. "Perhaps the chief task of economists at this hour," he said, quoting Bentham, "is to distinguish afresh the Agenda of government from the Non-Agenda; and the companion task of politics is to devise forms of government within a democracy which shall be capable of accomplishing the Agenda."[2]

If the distinction was important to draw in 1926, it is even more important in 1944. What is the function of American government today? Are we going to be able to dispense with most of it after the war, as so many hopeful citizens seem to believe? Or will it be more firmly in the saddle than ever?

These are large, fundamental questions which can only be briefly developed here. To begin with, it is fairly obvious that in power-age communities there are many essential tasks which do not appeal to businessmen as sources of profit. Running the schools, for instance. The government, federal or local, is the agency which does the essential jobs that nobody else can or will do.

Radio Waves

As an example, take radio waves. In 1927 all government controls were removed from radio broadcasting. Any enterpriser could set up a station and make it as loud as he wished. Bedlam ensued. New stations sprouted all over the map. Older ones in-

2. *Essays in Persuasion*, Harcourt, Brace, 1932. Some of the essays were written ten years earlier.

creased their power in order to drown out the new ones, grabbing whatever frequencies they liked. You could never be sure that a program clear today would not be strangled by interference to-morrow. People stopped listening in disgust. Sponsors concluded that radio was a fine way to waste their money.

Free enterprise had complete sway over the airwaves. After eight months of it, broadcasters stormed Washington, imploring to be regulated. It was the only possible solution. The reasons are technological, and cannot be changed by any act of man. There are exactly 106 radio channels, or frequencies, available in the stand-ard broadcasting band. There were many more enterprisers who wanted to operate broadcasting stations than the frequencies could accommodate. The government, by careful planning of wave lengths, districts and power, finally managed to squeeze in 900 stations.

To prevent chaotic conflict resulting from electrical interference, it is obvious that somebody has to determine who shall and shall not be licensed to broadcast, the frequency on which each station shall op-erate, the power of its transmitter, the number of hours it shall be on the air. It is equally obvious that the federal government is the only institution that can do this with any approximation of justice and satisfaction for all.[3]

Prewar Agenda

Perhaps the simplest way to estimate the future role of the U. S. government is to follow the trend curve. What functions did government exercise at a given point in the past? How does this list compare with another taken just before we entered the war? What functions does it exercise today, and what must it do in the period of unwinding from war to peace? What is the out-look for the long swing?

3. *Fortune,* May 1943.

Big Government

Let us take 1913 as the anchor for our curve. In that year the per capita cost of all government, federal, state and local, was $33.31. In 1941 it was $217.09. In 1913, there were 1,879,000 government employees at the three levels, in 1941 more than 6,000,000 — including the growing Army. In 1913 the federal government accounted for only 26 per cent of all government outlays, in 1941 for 58 per cent. Local government — cities and towns — used to be the largest spender of the three, and federal the smallest. In 1941, federal was by far the largest. It spent $13 billion, to $7.3 billion for local, and $3.8 billion for state governments. The total of these expenditures, $24.1 billion, was close to a quarter of the net national income in 1941.[4]

At this point, papers like *The Wall Street Journal* usually burst into tears and refuse to hear more. Let us press on, however. What were all these citizens working for the government up to — raking leaves, as the *Journal* fears? What were the Agenda of the State? Here they are:

Government Expenditures, 1941

	Federal	State	Local	Total
	(In billions of dollars)			
National defense	6.7	*	*	6.7
Relief and welfare	1.8	.5	.7	3.0
Schools and libraries	*	.3	2.2	2.5
Highways and transport	.3	.8	.9	2.0
Social security	.9	1.0	*	1.9
Agriculture and conservation	1.2	.1	.1	1.4
Administration and legislation	.4	.2	.6	1.2
Health	*	.3	.6	.9
Police	*	.1	.6	.7

4. Figures from J. Frederic Dewhurst, unpublished study for The Twentieth Century Fund.

Government Expenditures, 1941 (continued)

	(In billions of dollars)			
	Federal	*State*	*Local*	*Total*
Recreation	.1	.1	.1	.3
Interest and debt retirement	1.2	.4	1.0	2.6
Miscellaneous	.4	*	.5	.9
Total	13.0	3.8	7.3	24.1

* Less than $50,000,000. The table does not include government enterprises which earn their keep, like water supply, power, gas, postal service, port authorities, airports, and the like.

Here are the major functions of Big Government. Washington is chiefly responsible for national defense, relief, land and conservation outlays. The states are responsible for a large share of social security and highways. The cities and towns are chiefly responsible for schools, health, police. They also absorb a large slice of highway and transport outlays.

These expenditures originate in 165,000 units of government. Beside the federal government and the 48 states, there are 3,050 counties, 16,000 incorporated places — mostly cities, 19,000 townships, 118,000 school districts, and more than 8,000 special districts — water, irrigation, conservation, and the like. A magnificent streamlining job awaits us here!

Look again at the table. Granting for the sake of argument that the administration is deplorable, what function can be eliminated — schools, health, national defense, police? Clearly they all represent vital activities. Clearly businessmen do not see much profit in activities of this nature, except perhaps as contractors. These functions have grown in response to public demand over the years. No agent from Moscow started them. They began long before anyone was afraid of Moscow.

Agenda 1944

As I write, the invasion of Germany is in full swing, and Mac-Arthur is fighting upon the Philippines — where he swore he would someday return. In the all-out effort of total war, the federal government is in control of the whole economy. Little can be produced against the wishes of the WPB. Little can be bought without the sanction of the OPA. The government is spending $8 billion a month, close to $100 billion a year. It is ordering 60 to 70 per cent of all goods and services. Observe that the government is not making the stuff — except in regular arsenals and navy yards — but *ordering* it. Private businessmen are filling the orders.

Today, right now, in the midst of a dreadful verbal clamor about "free enterprise," "bureaucrats," "regimentation," those who have steady eyes can see the government men, businessmen, workers, and farmers linked together in one gigantic organism to produce such a torrent of munitions as Hitler never dreamed of.

Agenda for Demobilization

When the war ends I think we can safely predict that Uncle Sam will be thrown out of his total war position into something more modest. He will continue to order goods and services in the billions, whatever happens, but not at the present rate. The WPB estimates a 50 per cent cutback when Germany is defeated. After the Japanese war is over, the cutback will be deeper.

Reconverting the economy to peace promises to be more difficult than converting it to war. Conversion was done to an iron purpose; reconversion can become a purposeless scramble. To bring some sort of order into it and avoid disaster, the following things must be done; things that private business cannot take the lead in doing. They are service functions, not profit functions, and they belong in the Agenda.

1. Demobilizing 12,000,000 men and women from the armed forces. Congress has already passed a "G.I. Bill of Rights." The law includes unemployment insurance for veterans, subsidies for education and vocational training, the guarantee of loans to help purchase a home, a farm or a small business, free hospital facilities, and a speedy settlement of all disability claims.

2. Demobilizing up to 20,000,000 men and women from the war industries. Congress is wrestling with various bills, as I write. Millions of people will have to be transported over long distances, among other things.

3. Cancellation of war contracts.

4. Liquidating up to $50 billion of inventories.

5. The disposal of some 2500 government factories.

6. The extension of the OPA for a time, to keep the price structure steady.

7. The extension of lend-lease for a time, to stabilize our victorious allies.

8. The administration of relief abroad for a time.

9. The continued control of foreign trade and investment, at least until we know what other countries are going to do.

10. Control of airways and foreign bases as a military precaution.

11. The accumulation of stockpiles of strategic materials as a military precaution.

12. Control of the merchant marine for a time as a military precaution.

13. Controlling the *order* of reconversion so that industry does not tear itself to pieces trying to beat the gun to consumers' markets. (It promises to be a regular Cherokee Rush. The WPB is volcanic with pressure right now.)

Agenda 1950

When the world has stopped weaving around like the aspirants Joe Louis used to hit, some of these emergency controls can be dropped. For the long swing, what seems to be the shape of the Agenda?

To begin with, we can move the 1941 Agenda (as shown on page 111) right ahead to 1950. Those major functions of defense, education, police and the rest will continue to be major.

Next we may expect to see some kind of compensatory economy in operation, where the government slows down booms and depressions, by the coordinated use of taxation, public works and social security. The British Tory government is all set to do this, and I think it probable that the United States will develop a compensatory model of its own.[5]

In addition we might anticipate the following in the 1950 Agenda, in some form or other:

1. A great housing program, with federal aid.
2. Extension of present social security provisions to the whole population.
3. A great health program added to social security.
4. A nationwide nutrition program, and crop controls to reinforce it. The Food Stamp Plan of Milo Perkins, as well as school lunches, will probably be back in the Agenda.
5. More multiple-purpose river developments like the TVA. The *St. Louis Post Dispatch,* as a result of the disastrous floods of 1944, is now roaring for a Missouri Valley Authority, and Senator Murray has introduced a bill in Congress.
6. Large public works — such as continental super-highways, a national reforestation program, reconstruction of cities — on a scale hitherto unknown.
7. New and effective methods for controlling monopolies, and for checking conspiracies to restrict output.
8. Improved government machinery, permitting the Republic effectively to meet problems rather than to dodge them.

5. One model was outlined in the previous book in this series, *Where's the Money Coming From?*. Beardsley Ruml has released (July 1944) another model. Wendell Willkie advocated another in June 1944. *Fortune* proposed a model as early as 1942.

9. More government control of foreign trade and investment than in 1940, though not so much as in 1944.

All the above seem to be on the trend curve. In the next chapter we will examine numbers 7 and 8 in more detail. In *Goals for America,* the first six items were examined.

Deadlock

Here we are with a quarter of the whole national effort on the government Agenda before the war, and the prospect of more than that after the war. The functions involved are of the first importance. Private enterprise does not want to be responsible for them, as the outlook for profit is mostly nonexistent. Unless these functions are boldly and effectively undertaken, the whole economy may go swirling down in another debacle like 1932. Unwinding war controls alone is a most delicate and difficult task, calling for statesmanship of the highest order. Yet it is hard to approach the Agenda with boldness and efficiency because of our popular ideology.

We Americans, most of us, do not believe in governments — any government, and especially our government. We work for government, use it, take its benefits, would be lost without it, but we do not *believe* in it. So these vast and essential tasks start under a tragic handicap.

Geoffrey Crowther, editor of the London *Economist,* is greatly disturbed about this deadlock — which affects all the democracies to a degree.[6] He observes that full employment and social security are political imperatives today — as any opinion poll will show. The Russians and other authoritarian states can comply with the imperatives. That puts it squarely up to the democracies

6. *Foreign Affairs,* January 1944.

to find a way of their own. If complete free competition is impossible for democracies under 20th-century conditions, a highly regimented economy is no less so. It is not as efficient in satisfying the wants of consumers for many goods and services. It is incompatible with any degree of political freedom.

Hydraulic Brakes

So the democracies must have *both* free areas and controlled areas; both the profit motive of business, and the service motive of government. But it is very important to fix the zones for each. The deadlock comes in the marginal area between them. Those planners who want to extend the government Agenda on theoretical grounds have repeatedly held back business expansion, while businessmen and their friends have tossed one monkey wrench after another into necessary government enterprises.

Mr. Crowther is specific: "Risks of loss [for the businessman] have been increased by the great load of prior charges that have been put upon him . . . while his incentive to take risks has been dulled by heavy taxation, and his arm has been jogged by all manner of inspectors, controls, regulations, inquisition, prohibition and indictments." Government planning has often been negative; worse, it has been *punitive*.

The other side of the picture, says Mr. Crowther, is equally stultifying. Whenever a democratic state has tried to make headway against dire community problems, "it has been held back by a hundred visible and invisible strings of timidity and orthodoxy . . . every step is taken to the accompaniment of charges ranging from corruption to red ruin." The Liberty League hullabaloo in this country was an excellent example.

These restraints are like two hydraulic brakes, continually pressed down, under which the economy of the democracies has repeatedly lost its momentum. One brake has been at work suppressing the enterpriser who tries to promote something, and the other suppressing the "bureaucrat" who tries to perform essential public tasks. Both are stymied. *The problem before the democracies is to work out a plan so that the organizing principles of service and profit can both operate.*

The role of government in a democracy is to act as agent for all the citizens, superior to any special interest, and to undertake essential things which citizens cannot undertake as individuals. In our form of government the federal executive is the most logical agent. To represent the citizens effectively, the government should not only keep a tight leash on the pressure groups — a negative activity — but under power-age conditions it must act positively and aggressively in the interest of consumers, who have no pressure group to represent them.

The consumer interest is always the public interest. Every American is either a consumer, or dead.

11

WAYS AND MEANS

WHAT CAN BE DONE to curb the pressure groups, and end the recurring deadlocks which are growing so disastrous for us all?

Various partial remedies have been proposed. None of them is a cure-all, but Americans should be grown up enough by this time to stop looking for cure-alls. The first remedy that leaps to mind is legislation. "There ought to be a law." There is now no federal legislation regulating lobbies. Many bills have been proposed and all have been defeated. One sponsored by Representative Rowe is in committee as I write. Senator Black in 1936, after the Federal Trade Commission's disclosures of the power lobby, promoted a good bill which passed the Senate but was rejected in the House. The idea was to disclose the identity of the lobbyist and his employer, to prohibit certain people from acting as agents, reveal the money spent, eliminate bribery, forbid the payment of fees contingent on the passage or defeat of particular bills.[1]

Sixteen states have adopted laws requiring lobbies to register and furnish financial statements. "Experience under these laws has varied from success to almost complete failure." One trouble

1. TNEC Monograph No. 26, 1941.

is that lobby laws generally contain "no satisfactory definition of what constitutes legitimate lobbying."

Publicity could be a powerful safeguard. There are always some Washington newspapermen who take their responsibility seriously and expose Me First campaigns whenever they can. These reporters need the vigilance of a detective, the adroitness of a lawyer and the courage of a crusader. They may lose their social popularity or even their jobs; they run a constant risk of libel suits. Some of them meet the test, but there is room for far more publicity.

Organizations of consumers and white-collar workers can accomplish a good deal. Kenneth Crawford calls them "the most hopeful developments of the last few years." Here is a point where the individual citizen can lend a hand, joining consumer groups and cooperatives. Two recent developments have given the consumer movement a great impetus — first and chiefly the OPA, with its ceiling prices and encouragement to customers, housewives and plain citizens; second, those labor organizations which have acted as gadfly to the OPA. The cost-of-living figures of the CIO were severely criticized on technical grounds, but the effect was to express a strong political demand for price control.

The OPA is an example of government representation for an economic group, even though that group comprises the entire population. In practice it is people in the lower brackets that receive most protection, as they should. Whenever the government is able to give an economic group legitimate representation — as the FSA represented marginal farmers — it forestalls the organization of a lobby.

Other ways and means should be devised within government to give fair representation to economic groups, including commercial interests. Proposals have been made to select one house of Congress on occupational lines instead of geographical. The aim here would be to give due weight to all of them and undue power to none. The idea is worth study by qualified political scientists. It would require, of course, a Constitutional amendment.

Controlling Monopoly

Turning to the urgent problem of controlling monopoly, what methods have been proposed for that? We have seen many examples of how uncontrolled monopolies, whether of businessmen, workers or farmers, can seriously hurt modern communities. If some folks refuse to produce, other folks are going to suffer. Even if the goods can be spared, the purchasing power cannot. If restriction of output is widespread, the whole economy begins to lose its balance.

Furthermore, as pointed out earlier, inflexible prices and other monopolistic practices might well make it impossible to get full employment through compensatory fiscal devices. As fast as the government closed the dollar circuit, the monopolies could open gaps in it again. This might result in an uncontrolled inflation, as the Treasury threw its dollars into a bottomless pit.

William L. Batt, head of SKF Industries, president of the National Planning Association, and a high official of the WPB, delivered a solemn warning to fellow businessmen:[2]

Business will largely determine the size of the [postwar] demand, depending on whether it goes on a high-priced line or a low-priced line. I have already indicated, in advancing the program of more goods for more people at lower prices, that the National Planning Association believes the tendency of business must be toward lower and lower price levels.

2. Testimony before the House Committee on Post War Planning, April 13, 1944.

Mr. Batt in effect comes out for the Dollar Watch formula —
one excellent remedy for the worst evil of monopoly. Wherever
monopolies jack up price levels, choke off demand, block the machines from running, they should be blasted out of the way.
Where they aid the machines to run better, they should be en-
couraged. In the case of a power grid, a monopoly helps the machines; a tangle of competing transmission lines makes no sense.
But if the power grid is so controlled as to restrict its service and
charge high rates, a little competition may have to be introduced,
such as the "yardstick" of the TVA.

A given monopoly should not be condemned because it is a
monopoly, but rather *on the basis of its actual effect upon the
economy*. Regular monthly publication of the percentage of output to capacity in a monopolistic enterprise would furnish an eloquent prima-facie index of whether or not it was slowing down
the machines.

If output needs to be restricted — and in an economy of abundance this can occasionally happen — the state is the only legitimate agent to do it.

Useful and Harmful Monopolies

A careful study should be made of monopolies which have no
excuse for being except greed, and those which are technologically
justified. The first can perhaps be broken up by Thurman Arnold's type of sausage grinder, under the Sherman Act, and
forced back into the field of free competition. I say perhaps, because some may be too big to be broken up without excessive social damage. The second type — where monopolies have some
real justification — can legally be regulated, like other activities
affected with a public interest. How? Here are some suggested
methods:

1. Make them register their agreements with public authority, and generally conduct their operations in a goldfish bowl.

2. Have public authority fix their prices or profits, as in the case of public utilities.

3. Operate yardsticks, like the TVA, to hold their prices in line. Here is where some of the war plants — say the aluminum factories — might come in handy.

4. Encourage cooperative associations to compete with them. This has been very effective in Sweden, where the electric light bulb trust was broken.

5. Encourage little business to compete by making capital cheap, or by giving little business priorities in operating war plants, or both.

6. Revise the patent law so that great corporations cannot tie up an industry to perpetuity, entangling all newcomers in the hopeless barbed wire of infringement suits.

7. Enforce output quotas by public authority in cases where a monopoly shows signs of going quietly to sleep at 50 per cent of capacity.

8. Require the federal incorporation of companies.

Finally, and as a last resort, if a monopoly cannot be brought to serve the public interest by any of these regulatory methods, then the government should take over full control.

There seems to be no escape from this logic. We might put it in the form of a syllogism.

Monopolies restrict output.
Irresponsible restriction of output is intolerable in modern societies.
Therefore monopolies must be controlled. The only legitimate power to do this is the state.

The alternative would seem to be an increasing rigidity, until the economy cracked apart. At which point, in not a few modern countries, a dictator has taken over, and the state has intervened in far more unpleasant forms. People who insist that we must have fewer monopolies and at the same time less government interference, seem to be arguing in circles.

Some Medicine for Unions

Labor unions are in effect monopolies in the labor market. They prevent wages from falling according to the unfettered play of supply and demand. If the unions manipulate the wage structure in the interest of restriction of output, preventing the performance of work which needs to be done, or crowding two men on a job which one can readily do, public opinion may come down on them harder than on big business monopolies. Unions as well as businessmen need to apply the Dollar Watch formula. By keeping wage rates reasonable they can often earn more annual take-home pay.

If organized labor will identify its own interest with that of the public, it has an unlimited future. This does not mean singing patriotic songs and letting collective bargaining slide. It means getting behind a program to hold the national income around $150 billion, and employment around 57,000,000 jobs. It means working with the Committee for Economic Development, if that committee has a similar objective, or with the NAM, or the veterans' organizations, or with anyone traveling that road.

It means getting behind measures for social security, medical care, broader education facilities, and decent housing, for all Americans. It means lining up for pure food and drug laws, grade labeling, better standards for consumers. It means carrying forward some of the exciting new techniques already developed for adjusting workers and their work.

Labor-Management Committees

The labor movement usually moves through three stages. The first stage is to form a union where there was none before. Leaders are fighters. Management fights back.

The second stage is collective bargaining. The union has been accepted as bargaining agent for the workers. Leaders are negotiators; most of the tough babies have gone. The tussle around the bargaining table is about which side gets the biggest slice of a fixed pie. Labor tries to get more wages; management tries to get more profits.

The third stage is joint action by workers and managers to increase output, improve quality, reduce waste, and so make *a bigger pie to divide*. The consumer gets into this division.

The Amalgamated Clothing Workers and their employers, the B&O Railroad and their shop employees, have had joint production committees for many years. These have been isolated examples, however, in a turbulent sea of fighting, negotiating and collusion. But the war has suddenly plunged thousands of plants, employing millions of workers, into stage number three. All over the country, managers are sitting down with union representatives in an attempt to increase production and quality, and hasten the destruction of the Axis. There are now labor-management committees in more than 5,000 plants. They should be continued after the war.

Why Workers Work

The unions also have an opportunity to join with the industrial psychologists in solving the cardinal problem of factory work. As it stands, it is an unnatural way of life. "The sharp regular daily division between work and play is a condition that must have been virtually unknown throughout the long ages of pre-factory history."[3]

The studies of the Western Electric Company at their Hawthorne Plant, made over a fifteen-year period, throw a flood of light on what makes workers work. It is not primarily money; it

3. Barbara Wootton, *Lament for Economics,* Allen and Unwin, 1938.

is not nicely spaced rest periods, or fluorescent lights, or short hours, or a dandy gymnasium and ball field. *It is the sense that the worker is important to the plant, that society has a place for him.* Give him that and his output curve goes through the roof!

The Training Within Industry programs are carrying these ideas to foremen throughout war industry — especially through the Job Relations Training.[4] Three things plague the typical factory worker: (1) doubts about his function and place in society, (2) the frequent monotony of his task, (3) the frustrating effect of having a conveyor set the *pace* of his work and deprive him of bodily freedom. We are beginning to get at these problems, and find the rudiments of a solution. At Hawthorne, a vast interviewing program, where 20,000 workers spilled their resentments to counselors they trusted, has had encouraging results.

The unions are the logical people to initiate, support and push forward these new techniques.[5] They are the logical people to work out a practical plan for an annual wage, whereby the employee may accept a lower hourly rate in return for a secure annual income. The CIO Steelworkers are proposing such a plan as I write. A number of concerns have already adopted it in a limited way. I think it is probably as inevitable as collective bargaining. The principle is simple: Would you rather get $20 a day for 100 days in the year, or $10 a day for a full 300 days?

If such procedures were made a permanent part of the labor movement, Utopia might indeed be around the corner. But on the basis of wildcat striking, jurisdictional disputing, feather bedding, group pressuring, Me First and the public be damned, organized labor has a dark future.

4. See article by the author in *The Reader's Digest*, September 1943.
5. See Knickerbocker and McGregor, "Union Management Cooperation: A Psychological Analysis," *Personnel*, Vol. 19, No. 3, 1942.

Family-Sized Farms

Most individual farmers do not believe that their interests should surpass those of any other group, or that they should be able to hold up Congress for special dispensations at will. They believe that they have had a tough break in the past — true; and will have another after the war unless someone gives them a hand. Again true. But if they are going to depend for that help on the farm bloc in Congress and the Farm Bureau Federation, they had better exert some rank-and-file control over them.

A long-range reform would correct the situation in Congress which allows a minority of citizens to control a majority of senators. A more immediate measure would be to divorce the Farm Bureau Federation from the County Agents' offices. As the only authorities which could do this are Congress again and the Department of Agriculture, the outlook is not any too radiant.

The best referent for the "American way" is not the little businessman, a comparative newcomer, but the family farm which started just back of Plymouth Rock in 1620. The skids are under it now, with the Farm Bureau and the Associated Farmers lined up for the big commercial outfits. If the family-sized farm is to be saved, together with the way of life it stands for, some pretty strong medicine is needed.

The Farm Security Administration, or something like it, must continue to encourage self-reliance by helping the small farmer to help himself. Furthermore he will need cooperatives on both sides of him — cooperative buying of fertilizers, feeds, farm machinery; cooperative marketing to protect him from the organized middlemen. He must also have access to conservation programs where he can join with his fellow farmers up and down the creek to hold and enrich his soil. *He cannot go it alone.*

The above is the minimum program of the two good men who

operate family-sized farms in Pennsylvania.[6] I think they know what they are talking about. I think something like this must be done, if the family farm is not to fall into tenantry or worse. For agriculture as a whole, as we said before, the biggest single reform would be the war demand carried over into the peace by full employment. When workers have jobs farmers have prosperity.

The Constructive Note

We have touched on only a few of the remedies proposed for a better ordering of pressure groups after the war. What is needed even more than remedial plans at this stage is competent analysis, an authoritative survey to show who is responsible for what in this humming, complicated power age.

We need to know what the logical place of government should be in a 1950 political democracy. What is the logical field for businessmen, for the cooperatives, for the nonprofit services? We need to know specifically why the machinery of our federal government is often so close to the breaking point. A detailed survey along this line has never been attempted.[7] If we had one today, constructive plans would be easier to formulate. There would be firm ground under our feet.

But most of all we need a realization that our personal interest is bound up with the national interest. So long as most of us are concentrated on the main chance, deadlock is likely to succeed deadlock.

The Committee for Economic Development is a group of businessmen committed to a program of high employment after the war. Their goal is 55 to 57 million jobs. This shows commendable

6. Waring and Teller, *Roots in the Earth,* Harper, 1943.
7. The two-volume symposium, *Recent Social Trends,* McGraw-Hill, 1933, was the closest approximation. But a lot of water has gone under the bridge since then.

responsibility on the part of organized business for conditions which affect us all. It is an encouraging sign.

Getting Together

There are other encouraging signs. Here and there the pressure groups are getting together, not necessarily with the idea of a squeeze play on the rest of us. Before me is a picture in *Time* for February 28, 1944. Three men are sitting around a table in animated conversation — quite unarmed. On the left is James Carey, Secretary of the CIO, looking very earnest. In the middle is Ed O'Neal of the Farm Bureau Federation, with a benevolent expression except for a slight lift of the left eyebrow. On the right is Cloud Wampler of the National Association of Manufacturers, expounding a fine point to Ed and Jim. If there had been a GOD BLESS OUR HOME over the mantelpiece, the picture would have been complete.

The table is in a hotel at Atlantic City, where fifty-three delegates from sixteen national organizations have gathered to find an "area of agreement" in postwar planning. Others among the sixteen were the AF of L, the Chamber of Commerce, the American Bankers Association, the American Legion, the Committee for Economic Development, the National Foreign Trade Council, the National Grange.

The Big Three Make a Statement

In April 1944, a group of fifteen businessmen, fifteen labor leaders and twenty farm leaders signed a joint statement for the National Planning Association at Washington. They agreed that if soldiers return to sell apples "we will have lost the war." No economic group, they said, is self-sufficient; all depend upon each other. The terms "Business," "Labor," "Agriculture," lose their

capital letters and become "We, the people," when we realize
that "all the millions of us are consumers."

Each of the three committees then made a separate statement,
and I would like to quote from them.

We of the Business Committee recognize that management is dependent upon Labor to man the machines and provide new capital
from its savings. We recognize the principle of collective bargaining
as a sound and fair American principle. We also know that what most
men and women want for the future is a sense of security against unemployment, sickness, and destitute old age, together with a feeling of
participation. . . .

We of the Labor Committee recognize that Labor is dependent
upon Management to furnish the over-all "know how," to organize
technical and commercial research . . . and to attract from private
savers the new capital necessary to a sound and growing economy.

We of the Agricultural Committee in turn recognize that Agriculture is dependent upon Business and Labor; that there cannot be
profitable markets for our products except as the rest of the nation
prospers, and has the means to buy.

Among the businessmen were David C. Prince of General
Electric, Beardsley Ruml, Guy Emerson. Among the labor men
were Clinton Golden, Walter Reuther, Robert Watt. Among the
agricultural men were Thad Snow of Missouri, Donald Murphy
of *Wallaces' Farmer,* Allen B. Kline of the Iowa Farm Bureau.

I cannot remember anything like this ever happening before.
There seems to be no ulterior motive. The gentlemen have apparently come to the sensible conclusion that it is best to hang together, as the problems of the postwar world climb up the sky like
thunderheads.

There have been a number of similar conferences. In St. Louis
the other day, a large group of businessmen, city government

men, and labor men got together to lay plans for jobs after the war in the metropolitan area. So it goes. The very fury of the pressure group raids in 1943 seems to have brought this reaction, as if Americans felt that things had gone too far.

Perhaps you do not think these meetings amount to much, and perhaps you are right. They may be only a flash in the pan. But they *could* be of the greatest importance. They show an attitude of mind, a breadth of vision, a tolerance for the other fellow's interests, which have been conspicuous by their absence in America.

We cannot build a strong democratic society on laws and blueprints. We can build it only on people's feelings about other people. If the feelings are tolerant and informed, then the blueprints and the laws will work.

In his first speech in France dealing with domestic problems, General de Gaulle advocated an extensively planned economy. French exiles in London have been working on a blueprint for a mixed system, combining a sector of government ownership, a sector of government control without ownership, and a free enterprise sector. "In the first category would be all public utilities, to be operated on a pay-its-way principle; into the second would go key industries like metals; the rest would be free, with reservations as to labor relations and the exclusion of monopolies."[8]

European nations — or better, the continent as a whole — will have to be planned to survive at all after the devastations, migrations, shortages, property entanglements, of this war. It is even proposed that the United Nations should delegate a commission to direct the German economy for an indefinite period. Britain, due to her bombed cities and her staggering loss of foreign in-

8. Account in *The Wall Street Journal*, August 31, 1944.

vestments, must manage her economy for many years. Russia of course will be planned to the last thumbtack.

Only in America will conditions be favorable for maintaining a wide area of free enterprise, with planning confined to a few key points. We have the time, and the margin of national resources, to continue our institutions with a minimum of change. . . . Provided the American people unite in a program to level out the business cycle, underwrite a high level of employment, and bring monopolies under control; which means, at bottom, provided the American people learn to discipline themselves.

MOUNTAIN CONFERENCE

Sometimes I have a clear picture of the way the Agenda for 1950 could be presented to the people. I see perhaps a hundred leading Americans, men and women, meeting in some high, quiet place to prepare it. They are not the kind of people who are active in Me First groups. They are scientists, judges, teachers, university people, philosophers of business, lovers of the land, statesmen; and they think in terms of the whole community.

I picture them as people without ideologies or dogmatic principles, aware of their own shortcomings and the general inadequacy of mankind, as Wells put it. They are accustomed to approach a question with the scientific attitude, and to look at all the major characteristics of a situation before leaping to a conclusion. They are aware of the pitfalls of language. Supermen, if you like; but if there are not a hundred of them in the country today, America is in a bad way. We had more than that in 1787.

They ought, I think, to go up into the mountains somewhere. Perhaps the Navy would invite them to Sun Valley, whose beauty and remoteness would give them perspective. The young veterans recuperating there would remind them of the urgency of their task. They could look at the Sawtooth Mountains of Idaho, blocking the sky to the north, and remember the majesty and splendor of their country.

They could hold general meetings in the big Lodge, while sub-committees, working on detail problems, could meet wherever they pleased. Sometimes they might meet on the terrace of the Round House, 8,000 feet high on Mt. Baldy, at the top of the second tow, where they could look all over the Snake River Valley. It ought to clear the brain. The meeting should be held in summer rather than winter, with wild flowers, not snow. The delegates would do better to take their exercise on horseback, or fishing, rather than risk their tibias on the Canyon run.

I can see the Chairman getting to his feet in front of the big blue tapestry in the Lodge dining room to open the conference. He is a social scientist from somewhere on the Coast. His face is a little drawn, and he drums on the table with long fingers. He is no orator, but you can feel the whip of his mind, releasing something which seems to have been banking up inside him for a long time. I shall not quote him directly, but paraphrase his address, as I imagine it.

America, he says, has reached a milestone. We have met here to consider what we can do to help our country pass it safely. It cannot be muddled past; deliberate action must be taken. If thoughtful citizens like ourselves have no practical suggestions, the action will be taken anyway, by generals — or by demagogues.

The milestone would have been reached without the war, but perhaps not so abruptly. There would have been more time to turn around, but not a great deal more. There was not much time to turn around after the banks began to close in 1932.

The milestone, he says, is the point at which the pressures generated by a high-energy culture result in disastrous explosion under a policy of drift. In one sense, this war itself is such an explosion. Business depressions have plowed too deep; unemployment and insecurity have become too great, to be sat through patiently as one sits through a session with the dentist. The depression of 1929 was probably the last of its kind. It hardly touched Russia, which is an explosive fact in itself. It brought Hitler in Germany, the end of the gold standard everywhere, the Spanish Revolution, the Japanese assault on Manchuria, New Deals in many nations, and violent economic changes throughout the world.

As the depression deepened, governments shook off the rules of laissez faire and stepped forward to manage the economy directly — its man power, its money, its trade. In the process, many democratic governments toppled into the arms of dictators. Democratic legislatures had no plans to meet the crisis, or if they had, they could not act fast enough in their strait jackets of checks and balances.

The Chairman stopped a moment and leaned forward. . . . These are hard, unpleasant words, I know. But democracy is up against a hard, unpleasant set of facts. There are no democracies in the pre-1914 sense left in the world today. The war has forced even those few which still elect their leaders, far along the authoritarian road.

We who are meeting here, I take it, represent no economic interest except that of the consumer, which means everybody. We are not specifically for "labor," for "capital," for farmers, for organized medicine, for Wall Street, the West Coast, the export trade, the department stores, or for the manufacturers of Shocking Radiance perfume.

We are not in favor of "capitalism," "Socialism," "Fascism," "Communism," "individualism," or saving the world by the introduction of planned parenthood. We have gone through these vague ideologies and come out on the other side. We are in favor of keeping our minds open and the machines running. We want the community to go on, not to stop dead in its tracks as in 1929.

We are not prejudiced in favor of private business, government business, cooperative business or nonprofit business. We believe that each has its place, depending on circumstances. At one extreme stand the courts, which are certainly a function of government; at the other stands the aforesaid Shocking Radiance, which is certainly a function of private enterprise — with maybe just a dash of the Federal Trade Commission in the formula. In between, it all depends.

We have been called together to attempt a division of the "in between." A problem clearly stated is halfway solved. We want to run a line between the area where the public should be responsible, and the area where private interests should be responsible. Together they are responsible for 57,000,000 jobs.

We want to find out which monopolies can be successfully broken up into competitive units, and which cannot be without disaster. For the latter we want a program of control which will prevent restriction of output and keep the machines running.

We want to determine how far labor unions should be regulated in the public interest, and whether the Wagner Act needs amendment. We are sure, I think, that union accounts, like corporate accounts, should be a matter of public record.

While some of our committees are wrestling with such questions, others must wrestle with our disintegrating political machinery. If we had a government of Jeffersons and Disraelis in Washington, there is no reason to expect that even they would get far working through the present committee system of Congress, and hampered by the present division of fiscal policy and action into a dozen jealous bureaus. Because of the seniority rule, at nearly every outlet to Congress stands an old, old man, too tired to find out what the modern world demands. Such creaking machinery is ideal for the lobbyist.

We must have first-rate men in government, and public service made an attractive career to keen youngsters. We need a more enlightened civil service, better rules for tenure, many more schools of public administration. We need higher salaries in the top ranks, like the scale paid in England.

Our subcommittee dealing with red tape should examine the record of the Social Security Board. The Board conducts the largest clerical job on earth, with 76,000,000 Americans on its books. It should be a paradise for "bureaucrats." Yet in the two years after Pearl Harbor, it increased its work load one third, with 20 per cent fewer employees. How was it done?

David Lilienthal has given us an example of planning at the grass roots. The TVA works with the people of the Valley. It will not press projects, however excellent in theory, that the people do not want done. It will not undertake projects for the people unless the people take off their coats and help. I recommend his book to our subcommittee on the machinery of government. It is something new in the world. Young men arrive from China, Brazil, Russia, India, to study it.

We want to offer reasoned suggestions as to which public activities should be centralized and handled from Washington, and which should be decentralized and handled regionally, like the TVA, or by the states, or by local governments. We want to know why we should tolerate 165,000 units of government at all levels.

We want to develop some pretty clear ideas about the three major forms of government control: regulation, control-without-ownership, and outright ownership. Which is best for a given activity? In connection with the last, we should look closely into examples of government corporations. In many cases this form gets them out of politics and allows their managers to practice real efficiency. I see at least two such managers in this room. They can help us. . . .

These are some of the concrete matters we are going to take up, the Chairman went on. In order to handle them wisely, we must keep in mind some longer-range principles. We must remember that it is the era of abundance we are trying to adjust to. No nation in the world has yet solved the problem of distributing abundant production, except by war. This war itself has vastly multiplied our powers of production, so that abundance can be a greater threat than ever. We propose to find out how to make it a promise.

The wild horses of the power age have to be harnessed by someone, otherwise they will kick Western civilization to pieces, in depressions, revolutions, wars, struggles for power at every level. The critical question is: Who is to do the managing? The simplest answer is to turn the job over to a dictator. He calls in some specialists, exerts his well-known powers of divination, and then tells you and me what to do. If he is a benevolent despot, we may dislike his orders less than we dislike tramping the streets in search of work. If he is malevolent, like Hitler, many of us would rather die.

Since 1929, the Chairman went on, any expectation of free, unmanaged economies is academic. We all know that, in our minds if not in our emotional nervous systems. Men cannot return to free, unmanaged economies so long as inanimate energy and mass production dominate human activity. Furthermore, I do not know how many of us, when we get right down to it, would like the London of Adam Smith. We have to cope with the age that is here. To run away from it is to become impotent. The parade back to unlimited free enterprise is not an inspiring spectacle. It leaves young people confused and baffled. They want leaders, not retreaters.

Economic systems must now be managed. Have people in the democracies the brains to work out a kind of management which deals only with a few key functions and leaves most activities in private hands? The Swedes and the New Zealanders have done just this. They are small countries compared to ours, but experiments in a wind tunnel have often taught us much about flying in the open sky.

We have come here, I take it, because we believe our democracy can find the brains. If anyone in this room does not believe that a managed economy is compatible with political democracy and civil liberties, some mistake has been made in the invitations. That is one assumption we were all supposed to make. We do not have to assume its eternal truth, but without it as a working hypothesis we can do little here but toss a dilapidated ball of argument around the same old dusty circle. We assume that our democracy *can* manage its affairs, and we have met to prepare a temporary plan of management.

. . . At this point I picture two or three gentlemen getting up quietly and leaving the room. They are not again seen at any sessions of the conference. . . .

Americans, the Chairman continues, were not brought up to plan for, or even think about, their national survival. It was taken for granted. Politics they considered a gaudy sporting event, like a horse race. "Who is going to win?" was the great question: not what he would do to, or for, the country. A Presidential convention was written up by the newspaper boys in terms similar to a championship football game in the Rose Bowl. Brass bands and betting odds were central on both occasions.

People grabbed for things they wanted, and when the going was tough, they organized pressure groups to intensify the grabbing. These groups have grown so strong that they have distorted the whole economy. The idea seemed to be how much you could take from America, not what you could give to her.

Our forefathers set up an elaborate plan in 1787. They gave it a push and let it go. The expanding frontier carried it on for a hundred and fifty years. Lincoln had to do some managing, and so did Woodrow Wilson. But the New Deal marked the first time it was ever necessary to make over-all plans coordinating banks, farmers, and employment.

Now we are managed to the rooftree in total war. Everyone who stops to think knows we cannot unloosen those war controls without the most careful supervision, or unemployment will run wild. We cannot have high national income and full employment for the long swing without some controls. If the national income falls much below $130 billion, we cannot service the debt.

Preachers have long admonished us that all men are brothers, but they got nowhere in the era of scarcity when there was not enough to go around. Brothers sat on brothers' heads. The power age has given material foundation to the preachers' case. For the first time in history there is no need for brothers to push one another down. Look at the United States in 1944, producing twice what it did in 1940!

The economy of abundance makes the class struggle as old-fashioned as a high-wheeled bicycle. At the same time, mass production gears the economy into one organism, with intense specialization of work. A hundred years ago sixteen out of every twenty Americans owned their means of livelihood. Today seventeen out of twenty do not. Seventeen out of twenty are utterly dependent on the organism. Unless the economy is operated at substantial capacity, life becomes meaningless and intolerable for them.

Full employment or progressive degeneration is the choice we apparently must make, the price we have to pay for the fecundity of the machine. The enemies of society are not the rich who spend their money on luxuries, but those who restrict production and won't let other people work. These enemies are found in the monopolies of both business and labor. The pressure groups are crawling with them.

Many radical philosophers still think in the static terms of legal title. They want to divide property, strip the rich of their "ill-gotten gains," have the state "take over" the means of production. But in the modern world it is the dynamic output, the flow of goods, which is important. Idle assets, though the valuation figures reach to the moon, are worthless to the community. It does no good for the state to take over things unless it can move things. If the state can move things, it is unnecessary to take them over. The WPB owns nothing whatsoever. Just look at what it moves!

The Chairman paused again. . . . My time is about up. This isn't a speech but some ideas thrown out to get us started. A preliminary draft prepared by the steering committee is now before you. Each delegate has his copy. Your task is to round out this preliminary draft; take it as far as you can, as deep as you can, while holding general agreement. We want to obtain maximum agreement among ourselves. None of us belongs to pressure groups, but some of us have pet ideas. I implore you to drop them if they stand in the way of agreement. It isn't you who must be vindicated, it is your country. Broader still, it is democracy which must be vindicated.

We are sick and tired of hearing it said that we can never get anywhere because our government is so rotten — meaning, in a democracy, that *we* are rotten. We are sick and tired of running around in circles wringing our hands because we can produce so much. That is a game for people in a mental hospital, not for civilized men. The war has interrupted the game, but if we let things drift the mental cases will be back.

The question before us here is not whether there shall be government interference in the economy. That question was settled in the affirmative by the first administration of George Washington, when customs tariffs were enacted. The question before us here is what *kind* of government interference? Will it be to subsidize powerful pressure groups, or to keep all America strong?

The Chairman took out his handkerchief and ran it across his forehead. It was a hot morning in Idaho. Out the windows the mountains loomed through the haze, and the pine trees on their flanks looked green and cool.

I guess that is all, he said. Now we have to go to work. . . . And he sat down.

There was very little applause. The men and women facing him knew there was nothing to celebrate. A milestone in the history of their country had been reached. If it was to be safely passed it meant the hardest kind of work.